EXTREME ECONOMICS

The Need for Personal Finance in the School Curriculum

Keen Babbage

Rowman & Littlefield Education
Lanham, Maryland • Toronto • Plymouth, UK
2007

Published in the United States of America
by Rowman & Littlefield Education
A Division of Rowman & Littlefield Publishers, Inc.
A wholly owned subsidiary of The Rowman & Littlefield Publishing Group, Inc.
4501 Forbes Boulevard, Suite 200, Lanham, Maryland 20706
www.rowmaneducation.com

Estover Road
Plymouth PL6 7PY
United Kingdom

British Library Cataloguing in Publication Information Available

Library of Congress Cataloging-in-Publication Data

Babbage, Keen J.
Extreme economics : the need for personal finance in the school curriculum / Keen Babbage.
p. cm.
ISBN-13: 978-1-57886-563-5 (hardcover : alk. paper)
ISBN-10: 1-57886-563-8 (hardcover : alk. paper)
ISBN-13: 978-1-57886-564-2 (pbk. : alk. paper)
ISBN-10: 1-57886-564-6 (pbk. : alk. paper)
1. Finance, Personal. 2. Children—Finance, Personal. 3. Finance, Personal—Study and teaching. I. Title.

HG179.B233 2007
332.0240071—dc22

2006030520

∞™ The paper used in this publication meets the minimum requirements of American National Standard for Information Sciences—Permanence of Paper for Printed Library Materials, ANSI/NISO Z39.48-1992.
Manufactured in the United States of America.

To my teachers

CONTENTS

PREFACE

Decades ago, an enemy of the United States said, "We will bury you." That enemy failed. Current enemies of the United States need not attempt to bury this nation, because the United States is apparently determined to bury itself. We are burying ourselves with debt. Individuals, families, and governments are sinking under a ferocious avalanche of debt. When the nation succumbs to the debt burden, our enemies will not have defeated us; rather, they will own us. Our enemies do not have to fight us as long as we readily fight and resist financial responsibility. Our enemies merely need to finance our debt and purchase our land, labor, and capital. We will be conquered financially without a military shot being fired. We will have defeated ourselves through a series of unforced errors, unnecessary mistakes, and unwise habits.

The bold, honorable, productive, responsible spirit of 1776 that inspired the birth of the United States will have lost to a timid, shameful, wasteful, irresponsible spirit of financial failure and folly. Serious, sober, immediate, drastic actions taken now and maintained for decades could prevent this failure and reverse this folly. There is no time to waste and no money to waste. We face extreme economic problems that require extreme economic solutions.

The children and teenagers of this country have not caused our current and our emerging financial crisis, but they will inherit this difficulty. This book is for their benefit.

The United States faces a financial problem—no, it is a financial crisis . . . actually, it is a disaster; well, to be honest, it could become absolute melt-down. This is the time for many individuals, many families, and many governmental jurisdictions—especially, the national government—to take serious corrective actions.

America's enemies do not need to attack or terrorize the United States to destroy the American way of life. Our self-imposed financial irresponsibility could destroy this nation's integrity, authority, and future. While not in debtor's prison, we will be imprisoned by debt with no escape.

This fate is not yet inevitable; however, the likelihood of this fate increases with every passing year of individual, family, and national financial mismanagement. Solutions exist, but to end our addiction to debt will require withdrawal pain and significant changes. The options are clear and are opposite: Manage money wisely or mismanage money disastrously. The nation cannot endure being half indebted and half solvent. An individual's wealth within an economically and financially decaying society is compromised.

To every problem, there is an equal and opposite solution. To every extreme problem, there is an equal and opposite extreme solution. One purpose of this book is to help educate a generation of Americans by using the teaching concepts and topical content of extreme economics. Other actions are needed, but if the current generation of children and teenagers learn to manage money wisely, there is hope. The parents and grandparents of those students may need extreme actions to correct money mistakes already made, but the emerging generation can avoid the mistakes.

In 1983 the report *A Nation at Risk* was presented to the citizens of this country. That report concluded that the American system of education was failing so seriously that if an enemy had imposed such inferior conditions on us, we would consider it an act of war. States, school districts, and schools have taken heroic and historic actions in the past two decades to improve education. Those state and local actions are far superior to the national government's No Child Left Behind invasion of public schools.

The 2007 report that is needed would be entitled *A Nation in Debt*. That report would be a call to extreme actions to get the finances of governments, many families, and many individuals on a disciplined budget. Extreme economics is one part of the overall extreme action plan that can help correct the current and worsening financial mistakes that threaten the American way of life.

Health officials express concern over an epidemic of obesity. Too much junk food and too little exercise are among the problems related to excessive weight.

Extreme Economics: The Need for Personal Finance in the School Curriculum addresses the American obesity of debt. This nation is financially ill, sick, diseased, and obese. An extreme financial fitness effort is urgent. Let's start now.

1

HOW TO LEARN ABOUT MONEY

"We just do not have enough money for that. It costs $50 per person. So, with you, your mother, your sister, and me, it is $200 just to get in the amusement park for one day. Parking costs $10. Food would be another $50 or more. It's about 100 miles away, so the drive is another cost. Sure, it is a great place to visit, but it does not fit in the budget for this month. I had to get the car fixed last month. Your sister gets braces next week. We have a vacation planned for a week in July, but we just cannot afford a trip to the amusement park in June." Dad was speaking the apparently harsh truth to his 13-year-old son, Brian. Brian was disappointed but not defeated.

Brian replied, "I understand. Here's my idea: What if I earn the $200 it would cost for our tickets, plus I earn the $10 for parking, and, let's say, I earn $25 for gas. If I do that, would you and Mom pay for food at the amusement park?"

Dad was impressed. This could be much more than an enjoyable family trip to the amusement park. This could be a realistic lesson about money. Dad replied with encouragement but with his typical disclaimers and conditions.

"That might work. I have a few vacation days I have to use in June. Of course, you, Julie, and your mother are out of school, so your schedules are clear. You did say 'earn the money.' You are not taking money out of your bank saving account for this. So, tell me, how would you earn the $235?"

Brian was ready. "Julie and I already talked about this. You just might see a brother-and-sister business deal very soon. I plan on cutting grass in the neighborhood. Julie is going to baby-sit for families in the neighborhood. Since our last name is Moore, we thought we could call our business Chores by Moores. We already started designing a brochure on the computer. If you and Mom will let us, we'll start our business today."

Mom and Julie had walked into the kitchen and had heard the last part of Brian's comment. Mom entered the discussion. "Well, the business might be a good idea, but the first chores by Julie Moore and Brian Moore each day are done right here at this house. You know what is on your duty list for each day. Those get done before you do anything for a customer."

Julie had expected a condition like that. "Oh, that's no problem. Brian and I talked about our duties at home. We actually plan on getting up each morning at 8 instead of always sleeping late in the summer. By 9 or 10 we'll have our work here done, then we can make money the rest of the day. How's that?"

Mom and Dad looked at each other. Their smiles showed sincere pride in their children, who just might become successful summer entrepreneurs. Mom spoke first. "There are some limits. No working on Sunday. We go to church, we visit your grandparents, we have family activities then. No working after 10 at night, any night. You have to be home by then. The money you make each day has to be deposited in your savings account, except for, let's say, $5 per day, which you can keep for spending money, but you have to make more than $5 on any day for that to work. No, you have to make more than $10 on any day for that to work, so you save at least $5 daily."

Dad joined in. "It is June 4. Let's think of June 25 as the day we would go to the amusement park if you have saved $235 by June 21. Can you do that?"

"Of course," Julie said with the energy and confidence of a 15-year-old.

"No problem!" Brian added with total confidence. "Okay, Julie, let's go finish our brochure. If we do this right, we can make more than $235. Maybe we can even pay for all of the food ourselves. This could be a free trip for Mom and Dad, plus a great extra trip for us. Hey, do you think Robert could help us?" Brian hoped that their 19-year-old brother—who had just finished his first year of college and who already had two summer jobs, one at a tennis club and the other at an ice cream shop—could help them.

Julie asked, "What would he do? He has two jobs. He is taking a class to get started early on the next year of college. He's too busy to work with us."

"Not work with us," Brian replied. "Just give us ideas. He used to cut yards. Maybe his old customers will hire us. He knows people who need baby-sitters because sometimes his friends can't go places with him because they have to baby-sit little children in their families."

Julie agreed that Robert could be a great source of ideas. "Okay, Brian, now let's finish the brochure, make a lot of copies of it, and then take it to all of our neighbors. We'll make so much money that we could go to the amusement park for two days."

"Neat idea, Julie. Why go for one day when we could stay for two? Let's finish the brochure now and get this business going."

With encouragement from their parents, with ideas from their older brother, Julie and Brian could be successful entrepreneurs; however, they could have little or no success. The lawn mower could break and need a costly repair, or it could need to be replaced. The apparent simplicity of baby-sitting could become the reality of dealing with children who misbehave. The hours of work will bring in money, but when friends call to ask Julie and Brian to go to a movie or to swim, they will have to say no if they had already made a commitment to baby-sit, cut grass, or do other chores.

Julie and Brian, if they reach their goal of earning enough money to pay for the family trip to an amusement park, will learn many realities of business and many lessons about money while encountering frustrations, problems, and challenges. Some of those lessons often are learned through direct experience, but much about money, finances, jobs, economics, and related topics can be learned through study, reading, education, classes, school, and mentors. What advice could be shared with Julie, Brian, Robert, other children, and other teenagers about money, finances, preventing financial mistakes, wise actions to take regarding money, and preparation for the ideal job?

Later in this chapter, we will read the results of Julie and Brian's Chores by Moores business. They will each provide a business report telling the successes, the failures, the unexpected problems, the unexpected opportunities, the lessons learned, and the money earned. Will they reach their goal of earning and saving enough money to pay for most costs of a family trip to an amusement park? We will get that answer and many details soon, but first we will explore some research findings that address some topics that children and teenagers need to know regarding money.

Parents and guardians always hope that life will be better for their children in many categories, such as career opportunities, quality of living, economic security, and overall wealth. Recent facts indicate that, in some important ways, current adults are not handing a better world with better life possibilities to the current generation of teenagers and children.

The government of the United States, for example, has been on a rarely interrupted borrowing binge during the 25-year-period of 1981–2006. The national debt during that time has escalated from $1 trillion to almost $9 trillion. That is an example of how not to manage money. That is a debt burden that will negatively affect future generations, who did not cause that debt but who will endure the financial burdens imposed by that debt.

Far too many individuals in this country and far too many families have been on personal borrowing binges. Statistics continue to show how undisciplined the American mentality about money management is. When compared with many other developed societies, the average citizen in the United States is not saving money. Instead, one credit card that is used to the limit leads to a second credit card that is used to the limit. A mortgage plan could call for 100% financing, interest-only payments, or a 50-year payout. These actions create the illusion that people have money when the reality is that they owe money—a lot of money.

What is to be done? To every money problem, there is an equal and opposite solution. To every money question, there is an answer. During March 2006, I sought such solutions and answers via a mailed survey to a cross section of adults whose careers present a variety of work experience, whose educational levels are college or more, whose involvement in their communities includes many positions of leadership in job or volunteer duties, and whose judgment is respected. Participants ranged in age from about 30 to about 70. Participants ranged in career paths from restaurant owner to physician, from investment advisor to telecommunications technology expert, from local government management to college professor, from banker to dentist, from state government middle manager to corporate executive, from stay-at-home mom to heating/air-conditioning service technician.

Participants did not range in the quickness of their replies. Surveys were mailed on a Tuesday morning, and some were returned to me via mail by Thursday, an immediate response. I sent a survey to 45 people, and I hoped to hear from 15. I received responses from 29 people, almost double my expectation. A sample of 29 is not sufficient to claim scientific research precision, so this research is qualitative; however, the quality and depth of, as well as the insight and wisdom in, the responses add up to compelling ideas that demand serious consideration and call for serious action.

What financial guidance can current adult generations offer to Brian, Julie, and Robert? What money management insights gleaned, lessons learned, mistakes corrected, and conclusions reached are available to a 13-year-old, a 15-year-old, and a 19-year-old from people whose life experience has taught them how money works? We will now read the survey questions and some verbatim responses. We will then reach some overall conclusions. To conclude this chapter, we will hear Brian and Julie report on their business venture. We will also consider how the ideas from the surveys could be applied by Brian, Julie, and Robert, now and later in life.

There were six questions on the survey, which was introduced with a cover letter. A stamped self-addressed envelope was enclosed, so returning the survey to me would be convenient. People were asked to respond within 10 days. Most responses were well ahead of that deadline.

There was only one real surprise in the survey process. So many respondents added words of appreciation that they had been given the opportunity to participate, offer ideas to children and teenagers, help other people avoid money mistakes, and help other people succeed financially. The quality of ideas that people provided was matched by an urgency that their ideas be read, understood, applied, and followed. Those insightful, urgent ideas follow.

1. The most important advice I can give to a child or teenager about money is

- create a budget and stick to it.
- learn the value of money and always save some for a rainy day. It is not what you make that counts; it is what you save.
- begin saving early. Even a little bit snowballs over time.
- budget your money and value its actual worth to you. Ask yourself what money does for you and how you can make it do more.
- start saving and investing early in your life. Learn that discipline and then the rewards will come.
- learn how to manage money.
- compound interest. The power of 72 is an easy way for a young person to learn and understand how fast or slow money can double at a certain interest rate.
- learn the value of time and money—be aware of costs.
- save for a rainy day.
- save and pay all bills on time to insure a great credit score.
- learn the value of a dollar. Earn money to buy the things you want.
- get in the habit of saving as soon as possible.
- save, save, save. It's the key to reaching your goals in life.
- control your own destiny. Whoever controls your money controls your life.
- start saving early through a payroll deduction plan to get the power of compound interest.
- slow down and think.
- save at least half of every dollar you earn or receive as a gift in a savings account at your local bank. Get used to saving.
- do not borrow money.

2. Of everything I have learned about money, about finances, and about economics, the lesson that I wish I had known earlier in my life is

- save early in your life. It pays off later.
- do not plan for only 6 months, 1 year, or even 5 years, but for 10 to 20 years. Set a financial goal.

- make the maximum annual individual retirement account contribution as soon as you have an income.
- how to invest and allocate your savings and how to adjust that over your life for risk. Be more aggressive when you are young and more conservative as you age.
- how to create a budget and how to manage my money within that budget.
- impact others by giving your time, talent, and money.
- money is just money. Do not sacrifice your family, friends, and life in pursuit of it. Ten times more money does not make you ten times happier. Live a balanced life and be kind to people. Do business with people you like because you will be working with them forever.
- do not trust sales pitches. If it seems too good to be true, it probably is.
- the value of a great credit score.
- invest in higher risk possibilities like stocks.
- money is finite. It does run out. Have a plan B.
- balance your check book. It can help you avoid many problems. Living within your means is not possible unless you know how much money you actually have to live on.
- plan short-term and long-term goals. Just as you must budget your bills, you must budget your future.
- live on a cash basis only.
- other than your home, do not buy anything that you cannot pay for right there and then. No credit cards.
- pay yourself first. Always save 10%–15% of each pay check for your own retirement.

3. (a) The most common mistake people make with money is
   (b) That mistake can be avoided by

- (a) spending outside of their budget.
  (b) creating a budget and sticking to it.
- (a) overspending on items they cannot afford and/or often spending more than they make.
  (b) paying yourself first. Save it and forget that you have it. Learn to budget.

- (a) thinking money leads to happiness. Although it helps, it can also be the sources of much conflict and stress if not managed appropriately.
  (b) learning to find value in things other than material possessions.
- (a) spending too much.
  (b) understanding your "wants" versus your "needs." We generally want "stuff," which often comes with hefty price tags that stretch our finances and take away our savings.
- (a) thinking they have to spend more just because they make more.
  (b) rebudgeting any time your income changes so you discipline yourself to save more and invest more not spend more.
- (a) overextending themselves with credit and debt.
  (b) not making purchases unless you have the money to back them up.
- (a) spending, spending, spending.
  (b) living within your means. Do the math! Loans and credit card debt can never be paid off if you just pay the interest.
- (a) overspending—living on money before it is within their budget, such as reliance on "plastic spending" or credit cards.
  (b) learning to live within a budget.
- (a) not understanding money—how to make it, keep it, and double it.
  (b) following good real-life examples of people who successfully manage their money and who fully understand how money works.
- (a) spending more than they make.
  (b) budgeting wisely.
- (a) calculating how much you can spend with credit cards by your ability to make the minimum payment only.
  (b) never putting more on a credit card than you can fully pay off when the credit card bill arrives.
- (a) trying to keep up with the lifestyle and the spending of other people.
  (b) living within your means.
- (a) not knowing how much credit they can safely use.
  (b) having only one credit card and using it only for items you need and can already pay for.
- (a) spending more than they take in.
  (b) budgeting wisely.
- (a) taking on too much debt.

(b) living within your means. Live within a budget based on how much you earn, not how much credit you can get.

- (a) having too much debt.
  (b) learning disciplined spending and delayed gratification.
- (a) falling for the marketing and advertising messages of "It's cool only if it's new" or "If you want to belong to the right group, you must have the right product."
  (b) outsmarting marketers by being extremely frugal.
- (a) sacrificing long-term financial goals for near-term impulse purchases.
  (b) exercising fiscal discipline—for example, buy a good used car instead of the hot, new-model car.
- (a) buying on credit.
  (b) using a credit card only if you can pay it in full each month and only for items you need.

4. As an elementary school student, middle school student, or high school student, the smartest action you can take now about money is to

- make saving a habit.
- set goals—make a plan to get there and then plan the action to make it happen.
- get a job to earn money and you will have a greater appreciation and sense of responsibility for it.
- spend less than you earn. "Income" is not the same as "wealth." Manage your income by saving and investing as much as possible to create wealth.
- ask yourself what your goals are and how money can help you achieve these goals. When you start to make money, you can then budget according to your goals.
- start saving as early as possible.
- get a better understanding about how credit works, about when and how to use credit, about how to avoid credit mistakes.
- invest in yourself and in your education. Read about how to start a business and about how to invest money. Avoid "get rich" schemes. Learn about time-proven ways to make money safely over time.
- increase your awareness about money and realities about money.
- start a savings plan and shop around for the highest savings-account interest rate.

- never use a credit card until you are able to make the payment in full immediately after the bill arrives.
- set priorities for money to emphasize what is most important for you.
- make a budget. Open a savings account and pay it first whenever you earn money or are given money.
- learn to save. Have your family help you set up your own savings account at a bank and begin regularly saving some of your allowance or other income.
- begin earning money early in your life and then get in the habit of saving early in your life.
- not buy CDs, DVDs, or books if you can check out those items free at the public library.
- understand the concept of compound interest so you realize how to get your money to add growth to growth.
- save some for your education so you can get more education and become qualified for better jobs so you can earn more in the future.

5. To be sure that someday you actually get the job you dream of, be sure that you do this:

- Learn to write. If you can write, you can think. If you cannot write, it is difficult to communicate what you think. Writing forces you to put thoughts into context with a structure.
- Prepare by using resources such as guidance counselors at school and other mentors to advise you of the right classes to take.
- Be able to stand out in a candidate pool of 30 people to be interviewed for a job. Know why you should be hired and be able to convincingly communicate those reasons.
- Talk to people who currently hold the job that you think you might eventually want. Ask these people what it took for them to get where they are and what advice they can give you. Get experience in that work through internships.
- First, get the education required for the job. Second, be willing to start at the bottom and then perform very well so your results can be recognized.

- Find your passion.
- Research job requirements thoroughly and set personal goals so that you can meet those requirements.
- Get the best education possible.
- Aim high and work hard.
- Do not do the job for the money. Do the job because it is your passion.
- Get as much hands-on experience as you can through internships, volunteering, and job-shadowing. These activities help show potential employers that you have what it takes to do the job. Also, these activities can help you determine whether your dream job is really something you would succeed in.
- Find out what the qualifications are and get those qualifications through education, experiences, and training.
- Believe in your abilities. Do not let other people or your own fears keep you from achieving your goals. Attack your goals voraciously.
- Never give up on the dream, but be logical—you are not going to be in the NBA if you are 5'5".
- Always do what you say you will do and be prompt in everything you do. Do not procrastinate.
- Be 100% honest.
- Prepare yourself properly. Visit someone who is doing that job now. Get the required education for the job.

6. Please add any other insights you would like to provide about money, finances, economics, jobs, college, graduate/professional school, or related topics:

- Use common sense. Money is complicated when you do not have any. Save it and you will have it.
- Build a personal and professional network of allies. Have one or several formal or informal mentors who can counsel you along your way.
- When you set up your budget after you start working full-time, after essential living expenses, include your maximum contribution to retirement plans such as an individual retirement account. You can never have too much money at retirement.

- For every action you take, make sure that it is beneficial to you. Do not just have a good day; make it a good day.
- Think globally—the opportunities are unlimited.
- Finances and economics are scary only because we have created a mystique, but they are like anything else—understandable and manageable. Get the roots, the basics—and understanding the details will come more easily.
- I wanted to be a pediatrician when I was in high school. In college, I got a B in physics and decided that if that was the best I could do, then I could not be trusted with the life of a child. My pediatrician friend laughs at this. He says, "The only time I use physics is to unjam the copier." The moral of that example is, do not talk yourself out of your dreams.
- Take pride in your academic pursuits. Ask yourself this question in everything you do academically: Is this my absolute best work? If no, do it over.
- Honesty is integrity on display. Tact does not mean you are being dishonest. Tact means knowing when to be silent.
- When deciding what to do with your life after school, ask yourself these two questions from time to time: (1) Am I helping people? (2) Am I, in my work, my words, my actions, making this a better world to live in?
- Force yourself to understand the difference between "needs" and "wants." Discipline yourself about how to manage money. Do not blow money just because you have it now.

Take a few minutes, please, and read the survey results again. This time, as you read the results, think of the overall conclusions, themes, concepts that connect the survey responses. The survey replies came from people who did not compare notes or trade ideas; rather, the respondents worked independently yet reached some remarkably similar consistent conclusions.

Now that you have read the survey results again, what did you notice as the major themes, ideas, and suggestions emerging from the replies? If this is your book, please write your list on the following page; if not, please use other paper.

1.
2.
3.
4.
5.
6.
7.
8.

As I have read and reread the survey results, the following topics continue to emphatically stand out:

1. Save, save more, keep saving.
2. Start saving now, get in the habit of saving, view saving as required rather than optional.
3. Have a money plan, use a budget, manage money, and control money.
4. Credit is deceptive and potentially destructive.
5. Live within your means. Emphasize needs over wants.
6. Life is not about money, but if you manage the money part of life well, the other parts can go much better.
7. The measurement system for economics is math, so always do the math of money, including a budget, calculations about how money grows when saved and invested, and the ability to say no when the money math tells you to say no.
8. Get the best and the most education you can. Expand your life experiences through volunteer work, internships, and school–work partnerships.
9. Develop a strong work ethic in particular and an honorable set of ethics in general.
10. People are more important than money. Manage money well, and you can do more with or for people. Interact with people well, and better financial opportunities can come your way.

Julie and Brian's parents were impressed with the Chores by Moores idea, which their daughter and younger son created. Mom and Dad eagerly hoped that the business would be successful beyond what their children expected. Julie and Brian saw their business as a way to pay for a family trip to an amusement park. Mom and Dad realized that Julie and Brian could earn enough money for the amusement park trip; could earn additional money for other goals, including new savings accounts for college; and could learn many of the lessons about money management that can be helpful throughout a lifetime. If you learn the truth, facts, and realities about money at ages 13 and 15, you have many advantages.

Mom and Dad also hoped that Julie and Brian would learn some character education lessons. Chores by Moores would not be instantly successful, so persistence, determination, courage, work, endurance, and creativity would be needed. Unexpected problems would occur, and those would help Julie and Brian learn how to think, evaluate, analyze, and invent. The people skills used with customers would need to be impressive, or Chores by Moores would have customers who used the business only once. Starting, managing, developing, and maintaining this business could be vital parts of the teenage years for Julie and Brian.

What were the results? The best way to learn about the results is to hear from Julie and Brian. When the new school year began in August, Julie's 10th-grade language arts class had a paper to turn in. The students also had a reading list for the summer. There were several choices of topics for the paper:

1. Evaluate one international or national event from the summer.
2. Create a 3-minute script of a television travel show story about a trip you took this summer and include four pictures of the trip's locations.
3. If you had a job this summer, describe your achievements on the job, your duties at the job, and the lessons you learned from the job.

Julie selected the third option and wrote the following account.

We Earned It and Learned It

By Julie Moore

This past summer almost began with a very serious problem at the Moore home. After a few days of recovering from the last school year, my *younger brother, Brian, asked our parents if they could take us to Wild, Wild World amusement park. Dad said that there was no way to do that. Why? The family budget was tight, the summer schedule already included a trip, and there was one more really important reason. Dad said that the amusement park just costs too much. He thought that $50 per person was outrageous. Brian thought that missing the new Wild, Wild Super Extreme Roller Coaster would be outrageous, but Brian was smart enough not to argue with our parents.*

Brian asked our father the perfect question. I was really impressed with how diplomatically—there's a fancy sophomore language arts word for you—Brian handled the situation. He asked if Mom and Dad would take us to Wild, Wild World if we earned the money for the trip. How could they say no? If we earn the money, everyone gets a trip and our parents go at our expense. If we did not earn the money, well, that would be our fault.

My parents agreed. Brian recruited me to help, and I was actually eager to be involved. I like Wild, Wild World more than Brian does. I knew that there was money to be made in baby-sitting. Brian was sure he could make money cutting grass. We named our business Chores by Moores since we were willing to do chores and because our last name is Moore. Our parents gave us three weeks to earn $235 for the amusement park trip—$200 for the four tickets, $25 for gasoline, and $10 for parking. They said if we earned $235, they would pay for food at the amusement park. That was great, but the truth is, we set a goal of earning $300 so we would take care of all costs, food included.

My mother added two requirements. First, we had to finish our chores at home each morning before we could go do chores somewhere else. Second, we had to put the money we made into our savings accounts except for a maximum of $5 apiece each day if we made at least $10 apiece each day. There was a third requirement, which was to be home each night by 10, so no working late.

Our first week in business was fantastic. Brian made $80 cutting grass and helping one family load a big truck because they were moving to another city. I made $60 baby-sitting, plus I gave a piano lesson to one 9-year-old girl whose family had heard me play piano at church. That one lesson was another $10. We were so confident that we would reach our goal of $235 and probably of $300. We had taken in $150 in one week.

We each worked on four days, so we could have kept $20 each for spending money, including gasoline for the lawn mower, but we each just took $10 spending money. One week into Chores by Moores and we had a profit of $130. Wild, Wild World was almost guaranteed. Almost.

The second week was so awful. Brian's lawn mower broke. He had been given the mower by that family he helped move. They did not want to take it on the truck with them. It cost $45 to get the lawn mower fixed. It took 3 days to get it fixed. Those were 3 days of no grass-cutting money, so Brian had to baby-sit. I had more people asking me to baby-sit on two days than I could get to, so Brian stayed with twin 8-year-old boys on two afternoons. Brian would much rather cut grass than baby-sit, but we needed the money.

Brian took the boys bicycle riding. Their mother had said it was fine, just to stay in the neighborhood. One of the boys crashed his bike, cut his knee, and Brian had to deal with that crisis. Brian is a Boy Scout, and he had taken a Red Cross class in first aid, so he knew what to do. Still, I can proudly say that no child I was baby-sitter for this summer had any injury.

After 2 weeks, our total was $190. I made $60 profit plus $10 spending money the second week. Brian made $50 the second week, so he paid $45 for lawn mower repair and kept only $5 for spending money.

In the third week, we needed $45 profit, but we really were determined to make $110 and reach the big goal of $300. All of the families I did baby-sitting for were out of town during the third week. What was I supposed to do? All I could think of was to do what the name of our business said, so I went door to door in our neighborhood. I asked people what chores they needed done. People liked the word chores. *They said it showed I was eager to work. I cleaned patio furniture. I raked old, dead leaves from under and around a long, long row of shrubs and plants. I washed two cars. I dug up weeds from one yard.*

The third week was my best week, but I would rather baby-sit. I like children more than I like pulling weeds or cleaning furniture. I had $70 profit from the third week. Brian had a $60 profit during the third week. We were way ahead of the $235 goal and were over the $300 goal. Our total profit was $320, which paid for everything at the amusement park with $20 left after our trip!

Driving home from Wild, Wild World our parents asked us what we had learned from working to earn the money. Brian answered immediately. "It was so unfair when the lawn mower broke. I was so mad about that. I almost gave up, but I was so determined to get to Wild, Wild World. So I learned to not give up."

My answer was similar. I told my parents and Brian how difficult those chores seemed to be at first, but then they were really pretty easy. Raking leaves, washing a car, cleaning outdoor furniture are not difficult to do. What I learned is that it's best to just get started working than to think of endless reasons to not start.

By the way, Brian and I kept Chores by Moores going all summer. We hope to keep it active all year with baby-sitting, yard work, shoveling snow, and the other chores that people need done. Who knows, this might take us on other trips every summer and help pay for college. We earned our money and we learned about money. Hey, does anyone here need a chore done at your home?

Brian's eighth-grade schedule of classes was fairly typical for a student in his final year of middle school. Science, math, social studies, and language arts dominated the schedule. Brian had selected Spanish as an all-year class, while some students used that class period for a reading class or for a second math tutorial class. Each student in Brian's school took two exploratory classes, which included art, music, health, physical education, speech and drama, computers, vocational studies, carpentry, home economics, and study skills.

Brian's schedule included speech and drama. The teacher quickly checked attendance and then said, "Let's start. To learn speech and drama, we need to do speech and drama. You have 10 seconds to think of a topic for a 1- to 2-minute speech you will give in class. I'll give you 2 minutes to prepare your speech and then we will start your presentations. First, I need to hear from each person, one at a time, what your topic will be. It has to be G-rated, legal, and ethical, which is a fancy word for doing only what is good. So, we now start 10 seconds of silent indoor thinking."

The students smiled, thought, looked at each other, and when the teacher gave the direction, the first student in the first row spoke. Then each student followed in turn; the topics that the students mentioned are listed below. Brian's topic should be quite obvious.

Movies
Television shows
Pizza
Summer camps
High school
Football
Soccer
My trip to Canada
Cheerleading
Cooking
The concert I went to
Moving to a new house
Making homemade ice cream
Baseball
College sports
The Internet
Skateboarding
Making money this summer
Eighth grade
Tennis
The wedding I went to
Space travel
Our car breaking down on a trip
My dog
July 4 fireworks

The teacher was pleased with the variety of topics and that the G-rated, legal, ethical standard had been met. "Great topics. Now, take 2 minutes and make a list of the ideas or details you will communicate to us about your topic. Then you will present a 1- to 2-minute talk about the topic. You may use your notes when you talk to us. Your goals are as follows: to be heard, to be understood, to be interesting, and to look at your audience as much as possible. Any questions?"

There were no questions, but the teacher knew that the absence of questions did not mean the presence of understanding. She had two students state the goals for this project in their words while everyone listened. She then checked to be sure that everyone had a pencil or pen and a sheet of paper. With these procedures completed, the students began writing.

Brian's list for his talk included these points:

1. Amusement park
2. No money
3. Not in family budget
4. Money could be earned
5. Chores by Moores
6. Cut grass, baby-sit
7. Lawn mower broke
8. Go around neighborhood
9. Made enough money
10. Saved money
11. Still in business to make more money and save more money

Brian eagerly volunteered to be the first speaker. He confidently walked to the speaker's podium at the front of the class. He glanced at his notes, looked directly at the teacher, and began.

"Early in the summer, I asked my parents if we could go to the Wild, Wild World amusement park. They said no, and the reasons they gave were the typical reasons parents give: 'It costs too much. We don't have time. We're taking another trip later. We can't afford a trip to the amusement park. It's not in the budget.'

"So, I told them that I would earn the money and pay for our family to go to Wild, Wild World. When I said that, everything changed. Suddenly, my father had a vacation day he could use. My parents even agreed to pay for food at the park if I paid for tickets, gasoline, and parking. Deal.

"My sister, Julie, wanted to go to the park, so she teamed up with me to earn money. We decided that cutting grass and baby-sitting were our best ways to make money. We had three weeks to earn $235.

"The first week was great, but then my lawn mower broke. It cost a lot of money to get it fixed and I had to pay for it. Then my sister's babysitting stopped for a week when the families she helped were out of town. She went door-to-door offering to do chores. It worked, and we kept making money.

"By the day we had set up as the decision day, we had earned about $300. We went to the amusement park and paid for everything. We're still in business and will keep working all year. We are saving money for a two-day trip next summer to Wild, Wild World, and we started college saving accounts. So if you know of anyone who needs work done at their house, tell them about Chores by Moores."

As Brian returned to his desk, the students applauded, and the teacher's smile was radiant. "Excellent presentation, Brian. Very thorough details. Lots of energy and enthusiasm. You started us off very well. Great work, now, who would like to go next? Good, Samantha, then Matthew, then Andy, then John and Nicole. We may do more today, but we'll get to everyone by tomorrow."

Brian's speech and drama teacher talked to Brian's math teacher about the presentation of the Chores by Moores business. The math teacher saw much potential for math problems from the amusement park trip and the money-making business. Brian answered some questions his math teacher asked. The next day, Brian's class did amusement park math and money math. The students worked harder on this and learned more from this than any textbook math, plus they saw connections between real life and math. They were surprised to see that two classes—speech and drama plus math—could connect rather than just be two separate subjects that existed alone.

The home economics teacher heard about Chores by Moores when the math teacher talked about it at lunch. The home economics teacher designed a project for the eighth-grade class to create real businesses that they could actually start and make money from. Arrangements were made for Brian to meet with the home economics teacher and film an interview about his business, and then the teacher showed that interview to her classes. What began as a way for Brian and Julie to earn money to pay for a family trip to the amusement park was growing into some very effective activities at school for several classes and many students. Ideas are powerful. These students are learning about money in ways that are real, personal, meaningful, and easily put into action.

Students bring life experiences to school with them; however, those life experiences are not always used as an educational resource. The next chapter further explores how effectively the life experiences of students could be used to help them learn what the research indicates that children and teenagers need to know about money.

2

STUDENT LIFE EXPERIENCE AS A POWERFUL CLASSROOM RESOURCE

"I just finished my lifeguard training. I passed all of the tests. I'm certified to be a lifeguard. I've already applied for a job, and they really need lifeguards, so I might get to work all summer at a pool. That would be so cool. I'm going to use some of the money to start my IRA before the end of summer. I'm just 15 years old. I'll have so much money when I retire."

When a student in our eighth-grade economics class told everyone in the class about his summer job and his saving plan, heads turned. The other students were genuinely impressed with the ambition, eagerness, plan, determination, and confidence of their 15-year-old friend. Jealousy and resentment were not expressed or sensed; rather, the other students asked for details. They had been taught how an IRA works, and they expected to have an individual retirement account started no later than age 22 or 23, but now they were thinking differently, more boldly, more wisely. Now they were asking themselves how they could match their friend's plan with their own jobs and their own IRAs.

For several minutes I listened to and guided the class discussion as students asked the soon-to-be lifeguard all about the training he was receiving, the job application process, the hourly wage, and how he would set up his IRA. Their lively, enthusiastic, purposeful, wholesome curiosities were leading them to much deep learning, to much personal challenge, and to new resolve.

We discussed proper ways that they could make money now. We had long ago done the math of an IRA, savings accounts, certificates of deposit, stocks, and bonds. The students understood the facts and wisdom of these topics. They created a list of ways to make money at their current age of 14 or 15. They knew that all recommendations and ideas had to be G-rated, legal, and ethical. Their list was practical and included the following ideas:

- Cut grass
- Baby-sit
- Walk dogs
- Wash cars
- Collect mail and newspapers for people when they are out of town
- Design websites
- Teach people how to use computers
- Run errands for people—walk or bike ride to shop, make deliveries, take brochures door-to-door

Some of the students had already done some of those jobs in earlier summers or throughout a year. A few told of successes, while one told of problems that some baby-sitting placements can include. When we discussed what was required to be successful in these jobs, the students had immediate answers.

- Show up to be there when you promise to be there.
- If you baby-sit, find out what the children are allowed to do and not allowed to do. If you don't, some children will say they are allowed to do everything.
- Always ask if there is anything else you can do. It shows how helpful you want to be.
- Dress correctly.
- Don't goof off. Don't spend time calling friends on your cell phone.
- Speak properly and politely.
- Do the job better than people expect you to. Look for little extra ways to help, like, if you cut grass be sure to sweep the sidewalks.

- Ask people if they know of anyone else who needs you to work. One job can lead to more jobs.
- Follow the instructions people give you. Do what they tell you to do.

The students know how to succeed in a job. Their list of what to do and what not to do could apply to jobs for 14-year-olds or 15-year-olds as well as jobs that adults have. We discussed these similarities. The students were impressed that the actions that could help cause success in baby-sitting or cutting grass were actions that could help cause success in their future jobs.

I asked the students how to apply these actions that help create job success to their responsibilities at school. The classroom became absolutely silent. I let the silence continue because it was obvious that the students were thinking seriously about an idea in the revelation category. One student smiled, raised her hand, and was called on.

"It's really the same. We do better in school when we are on time, don't goof off, dress properly, follow instructions, and do our work better than we are expected to. It's like school is our job."

When a student speaks such potent words of wisdom, the desired conclusion has been reached. The other students listened attentively to her and knew that she spoke the truth. Our next test had an essay question about the similarities of succeeding in school and succeeding in a job done for money. The students did brilliant work on that test. Their ideas, their life experience, and our work in class was real to them and highly productive.

The life experience of one student who had learned much and accomplished much in the process of training, applying, interviewing, and being hired for the job of swimming pool lifeguard was an effective teaching and learning resource. His story inspired high-quality thinking by other students whose life experiences in various jobs became the basis for a discussion of how to succeed in jobs that are currently available to students, how to succeed in future jobs, and how to succeed in school. Using the wholesome knowledge, interests, and talents of students as instructional resources in the classroom helps create a student–teacher partnership in which everyone invests effort; therefore, everyone is personally involved in and dedicated to the results.

Could the same process work with an elementary school student and with a high school student? Let's hear from an 8-year-old and a 17-year-old to answer that question.

"Ms. Brown. Ms. Brown. You'll never guess what happened. It was so neat."

Ms. Brown was busy organizing some materials before her third graders would begin class today, but she would easily finish her tasks and listen to Kim. "Tell me all about it, Kim."

"Well, two days ago, on Saturday, my grandmother and my grandfather came to visit at my house. We always have the best time. So, after lunch my mother and my grandmother went outside to work in the garden. My father had to take my brother, Chris, to a soccer game. Chris is 12 and he's a great soccer player. So, my grandfather and I started talking about the old times, when my grandfather was my age, 8 years old."

"I'm sure it was really interesting to hear about when he was 8 years old. What interested you the most?" Ms. Brown asked.

"Well, it was how he made money. And how much—or, really, how little—money he made, but it wasn't really little, he said, because money was worth more then. My grandfather told me that 50 years ago, a dollar was really worth a dollar."

Ms. Brown smiled and replied, "That is something we could use in our math lesson today. We could take prices from years ago and calculate the changes with today's prices. Great idea, Kim."

"Thank you. So, my grandfather grew up on a farm. When he was 8 years old, he had a lot of work to do to help on the farm. His favorite day was Saturday because that was when everyone went into town. Farmers brought all kinds of food to sell. Whatever they grew on the farm, they brought to the town to sell. People would talk, buy, look around, and make it an all-day activity. It sounded like so much fun. I wished I could do something like that. Then my grandfather told me I could do something like that."

Ms. Brown was increasingly impressed with the story that Kim was telling. Kim spoke with such excitement and such detail. Ms. Brown said, "Kim, we just might have you tell this story to the whole class. I can see a language arts project where everyone hears your story and writes a similar experience they have had or write what they think could be a continuation of your story. Please, keep going."

Kim was thrilled that Ms. Brown was taking her story so seriously. "Then my grandfather and I went out to the garden where my mother and my grandmother were. The garden is not a farm, but it is a pretty big garden. Tomatoes, corn, flowers, and a lot more. I offered to help, and Mom put me to work immediately. Then I asked if I could sell some of the garden tomatoes, corn, and flowers. I said I would go door-to-door in our neighborhood. Everyone liked my idea. We put some garden products in a picnic basket and talked about what prices to charge people. I started going from house to house. My grandfather walked with me. After going to seven houses, we had sold everything. I had $22 in cash. We had agreed that since it is Mom's garden, she would get half of the money and I would get the other half. I made $11, Ms. Brown. I made $11 in just an hour or so."

Ms. Brown was very pleased. "Kim, you also made some great examples for us to use today in our math lesson and our language arts lesson. Thank you so much for telling me about your garden business."

Kim's life experiences as a garden entrepreneur became a classroom instruction resource for math problems and language arts writing activities. Other students contributed additional ideas based on their life experiences. Ms. Brown knew what needed to be learned by the students, and she knew that making the learning real by making connections with the students' real-life experiences would increase the results.

Ms. Brown also realized that the upcoming unit on economics she had begun planning needed to be revised. Ms. Brown had been given a box of economic materials by her school's principal. The principal, along with every other elementary school principal in the school district, had been given an identical "The Amazing Shrinking Money Mystery" kit, which had a money magazine for each student, posters, pictures, worksheets, tests, and an exact script of 10 lessons for the teacher to use. It looked easy to follow the steps in the teacher's guide, but, to be honest, Ms. Brown had to admit that it looked ordinary, superficial, and contrived.

These kits had been provided free to the school district by a local citizens group that was affiliated with a national service organization. The intention was good—to encourage and support the study of economics by elementary school students. The recommended method, however—that is, use the script and the materials provided in the kit—would just not work.

Ms. Brown had another idea. She and her students would start a business at school. She discussed this with the principal, who agreed it was worth a try but who insisted that Ms. Brown at least use some materials from the kit because the school district's central office would expect a report on how the kit had been used. That was a bureaucratic requirement to fulfill an obligation to the group that provided the kits. Ms. Brown wondered if any teachers had been asked if they thought the kits would be worth using before the school district accepted the kits and obligated the teachers. Why, she pondered, do people who do not teach keep telling people who do teach, how to teach?

A few weeks later, Ms. Brown's classroom had economics posters and pictures all over the walls. She could honestly report that materials from the economics kit were on display in her classroom. She could also take much pride in the fact that posters that were made by her students were also on display in her room and that the students' posters about money, jobs, banks, and economics were much better than the posters from the kit.

Ms. Brown and her students did start a business. For two weeks, they operated a concession stand for 30 minutes after school. They advertised the new business to all families, all students, and all employees associated with the school. The after-school snack items they sold were determined by surveys sent to all students, faculty, and staff. Teachers were given 10-cents-off coupons to use as rewards for students who did great work in class. The coupons could be redeemed only at the concession stand.

The financial results were outstanding. The business had a profit of $178 in 2 weeks. The educational results were even better: Ms. Brown and her students connected their business to math and science. Just how is a candy bar made? she asked them, and their research showed the science of candy. Other connections could be made with social studies, language arts, health, art, and technology. Prior life experiences of students and the current real-life experience of the concession stand at school became teaching and learning resources for Ms. Brown and her students, to which no "Amazing Shrinking Money Mystery" kit and script could compare.

It was the Friday in August before the new school year would begin on Monday. Jefferson High School was a very busy place. The soccer teams, the football team, the cheerleaders, and the marching band were practicing. The academic team, the speech team, and the student technology club were meeting. All teachers were at school. Some new students and their families were meeting with guidance counselors to register for school. Custodians were responding to requests from administrators and teachers. In the midst of this vast activity, 16-year-old high school junior Tom Jackson walked into his U.S. history teacher's classroom. Tom was greeted by an enthusiastic teacher, Matthew James. "Tom! Great to see you. Welcome back to school. You're in my third block A day class. I'm delighted to get to be your teacher again."

"Me, too, Mr. James. Your ninth-grade civics class was the best. That's actually why I stopped by today. I know you are busy, but this summer was so great I just had to tell you."

Mr. James stopped what he had been doing. "Tom, I'm never that busy. Tell me about you and about your summer."

"Thanks, Mr. James. Oh wait, it's Dr. James, isn't it? I heard that you finished your doctorate this summer. That is so cool. Congratulations, Doctor."

"Thank you, Tom. Now, tell me about you and about your summer."

"Okay. Well, it all began with your civics class when I was in ninth grade. We studied all about government. I got really interested in elections because you had candidates visit our class. People who were running for city council talked to us. Candidates for school board came. You even had some candidates who were running for state office talk to us. So, this summer I got involved in a campaign. I volunteered last May in a campaign when people were running for major. There were five candidates, and the top two vote getters move on to run against each other this November. My candidate came in second, really close to the person who came in first."

Dr. James is a constant source of encouragement for students, so he spoke. "Great, Tom. I'm sure the campaign staff and the candidate appreciated your help."

"That's just it, Dr. James. They appreciated my help so much, they hired me. I completely redesigned their campaign website. I update their website several times each day. I got the candidate's blog set up. I'm 16 years old, and I'm their campaign's assistant director of technology, plus I get paid. All of the student technology club work we did at school, plus your class, put me in this job. It is so cool."

Dr. James beamed with pride. "Congratulations, Mr. Jackson. Here's a question for you. One issue in the major's race is the city budget. My question for you is about your budget. What are you doing to wisely manage your income from this job?"

Tom was not surprised by the question. The ninth-grade civics class had included some serious, in-depth study of economics. "I do exactly what you taught us to do. I save, save more, and keep saving. Most of what I make goes into my bank savings account. I have car insurance to help pay, plus other car expenses. My girlfriend and I go to movies and stuff, so I pay for that. But mostly I save. I'll be in college in 2 years. I'll need all the money I can save for that."

"Very wise, Tom. Very wise. I'm extremely impressed. Anything else going on today at school for you?"

"Yes, sir. The principal hired a few student technology club members to work today to help the new teachers with any computer problems. I'll be here working the rest of the day, plus I'll do that for any teacher 1 day each week after school for 2 hours," Tom explained.

"Wonderful. I may call you for help this year with some new uses of technology in my classes. There are some amazing ways to use technology in our classes. When we mention an election, we can click on a short presentation from an Internet site of real candidates debating from many different campaigns in recent decades. When I need help with that, I'll know to ask you. Plus, you can help me find technology resources to use with your U.S. history class. This will be perfect."

"I'll be glad to help, Dr. James. Well, I need to go work, and you have plenty to do. See you in class on Monday." Tom smiled as he turned to leave.

"Sounds great. Congratulations again on your work. I hope your junior year in high school is your best year yet."

Students are real people living real lives right now. Tom Jackson's interest in politics is real. That real interest can connect with many classes he takes at Jefferson High School if his teachers will get to know Tom well enough to know his interests and will think creatively enough to design instructional activities that connect Tom's wholesome knowledge, talents, and interests with the school's curriculum.

Much statistical analysis is done of election results. Tom's math teacher in the statistics class could have Tom analyze voting results from recent mayoral primary elections and general elections. Tom would learn the required math skills, functions, and content not simply by repeatedly doing page after page of textbook math but by eagerly doing exploration after exploration of numbers associated with elections. The required math concepts and skills can be mastered via election result math statistical analysis or can be merely covered by going over math book problem after math book problem.

Books have been written about political campaigns, elections, and candidates. Tom's language arts class could include some optional reading. If a language arts teacher needed students to analyze how an author develops characters in fiction or builds a persuasive case in nonfiction, political literature could serve that purpose for Tom. Other wholesome topics could be read about to connect with the wholesome knowledge, interests, and talents of other students.

In any class that includes economics, Tom's growing expertise in website creation and management is an excellent example of free enterprise, the entrepreneurial spirit, how skills are applied in jobs, how to wisely manage income, and how to provide outstanding customer service.

Extreme economics is a member of the extreme family, which has included extreme teaching, extreme learning, and extreme students. Extreme teaching causes extreme learning and develops extreme students by constantly making connections between the wholesome knowledge, interests, and talents of students and what the students need to learn. In the extreme classroom community, extreme teachers thrive on student input and application of students' life experiences because that makes the teachers and the students partners in learning. The teachers learn how the current students learn. The current students learn the curriculum. Everyone wins.

In the economics classes I have taught to eighth graders during 2002–2006, I always knew exactly what the curriculum required the students to learn. That core content for eighth-grade economics was established, provided to me, and did not change during those 4 years.

How I caused the students in each class to fully learn the core content did change from class to class, day to day, person to person. The reason to change the instructional activity, method, or technique was to build on the unique strength of each student and on the unique collective strengths of each class. For example, one group of students was especially interested in breakfast cereal, so many of our examples, case studies, calculations, and definitions were based on breakfast cereal products. From competition to supply and demand, from risk to money, economic vocabulary, concepts, and factors could be understood by making connections with breakfast cereal examples, applications, and realities.

Another class was interested in snacks. From fresh fruit to potato chips, from candy bars to granola bars, from popcorn to pastries, foods that can be used as snacks became an example for every economic concept the curriculum required students to learn.

It would make no sense for me to continue using the breakfast cereal activities and examples year after year with classes of students who have no interest in breakfast cereal but who have strong interest in snacks, athletic facilities, shopping malls, travel, and salaries of various jobs. I apply the motivation students already have toward their existing wholesome knowledge, interests, and talents to create instant motivation to learn economics.

The long list that follows will help show how the life experiences of students, including questions that have emerged due to various life experiences, can energize a classroom, make learning real, make economics personal, make studying economics important now, and cause learning. I occasionally ask students to tell me something about economics they would like to know that we have not yet discussed or that we have discussed but they still have questions on or curiosities about. The following list shows what students have asked me to help them learn more about during the past 4 years in eighth-grade economics classes. As you read the list of questions from students, think of the many concepts from economics that could be taught by making connections with the questions the students asked and the curriculum for economics. Think further of activities that the teacher could create using the students' questions as the basis of the discussion, activity, or project.

1. How much money does it cost to start a new business about inventing new things?
2. Is a check as good to use as money so you don't use a credit card or a debit card?
3. Is there a limit on the number of certificates of deposit (CD) that you can have?
4. Do most people who put money in the bank save it or spend it in less than a month?
5. What investment options for an individual retirement account do you have besides a certificate of deposit?
6. How does the stock market work?
7. When can you start your IRA?
8. How can the United States be over $8,000,000,000,000 ($8 trillion) in debt and yet we keep spending more money? What will the result be?
9. How much would two shares of Microsoft stock cost? Is it a good company?
10. Why can't you put more than the limit each year in your IRA?
11. How many accounts can you have at the bank? What are they?
12. How do you mange money so you can't be taxed on it?
13. Why has gas fluctuated so much recently?
14. How do you calculate interest?
15. I want to find good-paying author jobs. How do I do that?
16. How do stocks work?
17. How do I get a lot of money other than what will grow in my retirement fund? How do I get money now, not just money I save for when I retire?
18. Is interest always a factor when saving money?
19. How would I make more money at my age (13) besides save, save more, keep saving?
20. How do you buy stock?
21. Can I invest at my age?
22. I want to know about gas prices, if the prices will be $6 per gallon one day?
23. Where do you go to start a business?
24. How do you pay for college?

25. May I borrow $3,000?
26. Taxes confuse me. How do you calculate your taxes?
27. What careers are the best for making high quantities of money?
28. How can you get into the stock market? What's so special about stocks?
29. What is the value of foreign money compared to ours?
30. Why do we use money?
31. Why do things cost so much?
32. Where is money made?
33. Why are there so many different types of money?
34. Who came up with money?
35. Do any countries use the same type of money we use?
36. How much money does the United States make a year?
37. Why are the presidents' faces on money?
38. Why are faces on the new dollar bills larger than before?
39. How long does it take to make money?
40. Where do they make money?

When one class had two guest speakers from a local bank visit our class, the students wrote questions for the bankers, and I e-mailed the questions to our guests a few days before they visited. This enabled them to address the topics of importance to the students, and it gave me some new insight into the emerging curiosities of the students. The wholesome knowledge, talents, and interests of students will change over time, so I make the effort to keep updated with their new life experiences, life questions, life curiosities, and life knowledge. The question my students had for the bankers follow.

1. How old do you have to be to work at the bank?
2. When did the idea of a bank come up?
3. What was the rate of inflation from 1900 to now?
4. What would it take to make a countrywide deflation?
5. In time of little money, why can't we mass-produce some?
6. If a bank was robbed, would I still get my money?
7. Can an IRA crash?
8. Would it be better to put your money in a bank account or in a CD for a number of years, say 3½ years?

9. What is the fastest way to get money?
10. Do/can you make a lot of money in banking?
11. Why do you have to be 59½ years old to take money out of your IRA without a penalty? Some people need money before that age.
12. Is there a way to recover from going bankrupt? If yes, what is the way?
13. Can you have more than one bank account in the same bank?
14. If you have an IRA and you die before age 59½, do the people you let inherit your money have to wait until a certain time to get the money? Do they have to wait until you would have been 59½ years old?
15. Do banks print any money?
16. Do you have to pay to get an account at a bank?
17. Do banks have their own stocks which people can invest in?
18. Do taxes go up or down according to your income?
19. How do you get the money that you earn from the stock market?
20. If you sell a stock, how and when do you get your money?
21. How big is big enough for a stock to be listed on the "big board" of the New York Stock Exchange instead of on a smaller exchange?
22. What stocks would you invest in and why?
23. If you were really rich and you had your own company, would you be able to buy stock in it? If so, how much?
24. If the company you own stock in goes bankrupt but then bounces back, would you still get your money?

One additional life experience that students bring to a class is time spent in the class itself. After a few days in class, some new learning has been experienced; some new knowledge is being created, absorbed, gained.

I occasionally ask students to tell me what they have learned so far in our class and what caused them to learn that. Sure, tests, discussions, homework projects, questions asked in class, and answers given in class help tell me what students have learned; however, I benefit from their direct reflections on the questions What is the most important fact or idea you have learned about in our economics class? and How did you learn that?

What is the most important fact or idea you have learned about in our economics class?

- Credit cards are a bad idea if you only mean to use them and not pay them off.
- How to save money.
- Save money by putting it in a bank so it grows. If you put money under a mattress, it shrinks.
- How to save money.
- Save. Save more. Keep saving.
- Save. Save more. Keep saving. Be smart with your money.
- The lottery is a scam and you probably won't win.
- Save as much as you can. Save. Save more. Keep saving.
- Save. Save more. Keep saving.
- Save. Save more. Keep saving. And to not use credit cards unless needed to.
- How to invest money wisely with stocks and IRA accounts.
- To save, save more, and keep saving.
- Save. Save more. Keep saving.
- Never use a credit card or you can face the interest charge. Save, save more, keep saving.
- Save. Save more. Keep saving.
- Saving money!

Please note: On the first day of class, the students are taught that there are three rules of economics: Save. Save more. Keep saving. Those three rules are emphasized daily.

And how did you learn that?

- By Dr. Babbage teaching us about savings accounts, IRA, certificates of deposit.
- By listening to Dr. Babbage about the rules of economics.
- Dr. Babbage taught me and it is easy to understand.
- Because we drill this every day.
- By going over methods of saving, what to do, and what not to do.
- By paying attention in class. By listening and asking questions.
- The rules of economics and from our discussions in class daily.

- He taught us how to save our money and when you save you win.
- Playing "Deal or No Deal" and going over it.
- By seeing different prices in the newspaper for the same thing.
- I learned that because before I didn't know that the lottery was so hard and I got my dad to stop playing it because I told him what I learned in economics.

The most important idea within this chapter is that student life experience is a powerful classroom resource in the teaching of economics and, for that matter, in the teaching of any subject. The connections between students' life experiences and economics are especially powerful teaching resources because they are so numerous, so real, so meaningful, so practical, and so applicable.

In addition to the life experiences that were included in the stories in this chapter about an elementary school student selling garden products, a middle school student becoming a lifeguard, and a high school student working on the staff of a political campaign, what are some other day-to-day life experiences of students that teachers could use as classroom resources in the study of economics? Let's create a list that I begin and you complete:

1. Going to the grocery store
2. Going with parents or guardians to shop for a car
3. Being at a park and needing money to buy something at a concession stand
4. Watching a commercial on television
5. Reading advertisements and coupons in the newspaper
6. Talking to friends about the price of tickets to an upcoming concert
7. Going to a bank to start a savings account
8. Being told that the latest fashion in athletic shoes costs too much
9. Noticing the price differences between name-brand products and store-brand or generic products
10. Wondering why the price of gas went up, why so many people complain about that, and why so little seems to be done about that
11. Listening to a radio talk show about money
12. Asking why the price of water and soft drinks sold in a vending machine just went up 25 cents per bottle

13. Noticing that some houses in town sell quickly but others are quite slow to sell
14. Wanting the latest pocket-size music playing machine but being told that you do not need it
15. Seeing how much some people save at a grocery store using a lot of coupons
16.
17.
18.
19.
20.

The fundamental issue of, and conflict between, wants versus needs is of essential importance in economics. The student who eagerly wants the newest mini-music player but is emphatically told that the new item is not needed is face-to-face with economic reality. This is life experience economics, not generic, distant, someone-else, textbook, or worksheet economics. Because students are real people living real lives right now, when their educational experiences connect with their real-life experiences, they are much more likely to pay attention, become involved, think, read, work, study, ask questions, answer questions, seek knowledge, and learn.

We have firmly established that students' life experiences are powerful resources for the classroom. We will now more precisely consider how to exactly match student life experience with what students need to learn about economics.

3

HOW STUDENT LIFE EXPERIENCE CONNECTS WITH WHAT STUDENTS NEED TO LEARN

Save. Save more. Keep saving. Those are the three rules of economics. Each student in every economics class I have taught is told on the first day of class a few moments after class begins that there are three rules of economics. Some students already know these three rules because they have heard from prior students. Each new group of students joins me in repeating and chanting, "Save. Save more. Keep saving." Within a minute everyone has memorized the economic montra.

When I ask former students to tell me what they remember from our economics class, the most common answer is, "Save. Save more. Keep saving." One student explained why: "You said it. I thought about it and it is stamped on my brain for all eternity."

Memorizing the three rules of economics is a badge of honor for the students. Learning how to implement the three rules of economics is a realistic challenge for the students, but they do learn how to save, save more, keep saving. For example, the students and I do the math of buying a car. We use actual numbers from current newspaper advertisements.

If a $300 car payment is being made for 48 months, the payments total $14,400. The students are taught to keep the car for 10 years, which means they have 6 years without a car payment. The $300 that used to be a monthly car payment now goes into a savings account. Rather than pay $300 per month to the car dealer, the student would set aside $300 into a savings account, which will pay for their next car. Six years of $300 saved per month totals $21,600, and that does not include interest earned during the 6 years.

After driving the original car for 10 years, the student can pay for his or her next car using some or all of the $21,600 plus interest. The student saved each month for 6 years. The student saved more and more, month after month. Now with a new car paid for in cash, the student will keep saving $300 per month for 10 years. The total will be $36,000, not including interest that will be earned. Even with inflation increasing car prices over these years, the process of save, save more, keep saving will enable the student to never again be in debt due to car payments after the financing of the first car is paid off.

After completing the math of financing one car, saving for future cars, and buying future cars with cash, one student said to me, "You make it sound so easy." He was right, and he was being quite honest. His life experience had shown him that money management is demanding and difficult. He could see, do, and understand the car math. It seemed logical, sensible, straightforward, and wise to him. Why, he probably wondered, did his family not manage money this way? Life experiences of students can and do connect with what students need to learn, but the extreme teacher—meaning the teacher who continually makes connections between the wholesome knowledge, interests, and talents of students and what students need to learn—must be prepared for times when an outstanding idea that hits close to home of a student may create some cognitive confusion. Truth emerges when ideas collide. My student was not doubting the wisdom of what he was being taught about purchasing cars; rather, his life experience simply did not include that type of thinking about money or that type of management of money.

I had been teaching eighth-grade economics classes for 4 years before doing the research surveys for this book. It was encouraging to read the surveys and realize that the most-emphasized advice about money that survey participants offered to children and teenagers was to save, save often, save as much as possible, get in the habit of saving, save aggressively. There are some permanent, timeless truths about money, and at the top of that truth list is save, save more, keep saving.

After mastering the words, ideas, application, and implementation of Save. Save more. Keep saving. the students have two more essential, fundamental tasks. First, realize the amazing, absolute, and available power of money earning money on money, or, in another term, *compound interest*. This math convinces any student who might be skeptical, because we do the calculations by hand, with pencil and paper, so that he or she can see and feel the action of the numbers. Second, know the required vocabulary of economics. We use many teaching activities for this, but one old-fashioned method—flash cards—is often the most effective.

The number $1,000,000 is written on the front marker board. The students are asked to "please raise your hand if you would like to acquire this much money." Every student raises a hand to signal yes. The students then hear me say, "It will take some time, years and decades, to be honest, but I absolutely promise, guarantee, and assure you that there is a G-rated, legal, ethical way for each of you to acquire $1,000,000." The entire class is concentrating with 100% attention. Their minds are active. Their questions are forming.

"Here's how it works. Laws in our country permit, even encourage, people to set up an individual retirement account. *Individual* means it is yours, you own it, you manage it. *Retirement* means the money saved and invested in this account stays in the account until retirement age, which the law measures as 59½ years old or older. *Account* means that you set this up with a bank or other financial organization, such as stock brokerage firm.

"For our example, let's start by putting $3,000 in an IRA at age 22, and let's calculate that it grows at 8% per year. The money will grow tax free because it is protected by IRA laws. Many other savings and investments we have can be, and usually are, taxed annually or at certain times.

"Let's calculate that our money will grow at 8% annually. That is a reasonable number based on interest rate history and stock market history. At the end of one year how much will our $3,000 have grown to? Well, what is 8% of $3,000?"

The students do the paper-and-pencil math to see, feel, and understand what the numbers are doing. I call on several students, hear the answer $240 many times, but do not go forward. First, I walk around the room to be sure that everyone has done the math well.

"Great, we now have $3,240. Let's see what that grows to after one year. Do that math, please." The students find that the IRA grew by $259.20 in the second year, which is more than the $240 it grew the first year. They begin to notice what happens with compound interest.

We then discuss the law of 72, which in economics is a math shortcut. When you divide the rate of growth—in our example of 8%—into 72, you find out how fast money will double—thus, 8 into 72 equals 9, so the original $3,000 grows to $6,000 in 9 years. We then complete a chart similar to the numbers in Table 3.1.

A student then asks a reasonable question, much to my delight: "But $96,000 is not the $1,000,000 you promised. Where is the rest of the money?"

"Great question and very good point. Let's add $3,000 more at age 23. At 8% a year, that money will become another $96,000 when you are 68 years old. What happens if you keep adding more money each year at age 24, 25, and so on?"

The looks on their faces confirm that the power of compound interest just convinced them, a classroom of eighth graders, to save, save more, keep saving. This learning moment has become part of their life experience that connects with, perhaps contradicts but still connects with, prior life experience, including times when money was spent unnecessarily instead of saved purposefully.

We then make a precise connection with their life experience as I explain the following possibility: "Let's imagine that a sixth-grade student who usually spent $1 after school in fifth grade each day to buy a soft drink from a vending machine decided to just get a free drink of water from a fountain at school. The student would save $1 daily. If the stu-

Table 3.1. Value of Money Put Into Individual Retirement Account at Various Ages

Age	*Value*
22	$3,000
31	$6,000
40	$12,000
49	$24,000
58	$48,000
67	$96,000

dent does that every day during sixth grade through high school graduation, $1,225 would be saved. That is $175 per year times 7 years. The person is 18 years old. During the next 4 years, while he or she is in college, $2 per day is added to this growing savings amount as the student skips a soft drink or a costly cup of coffee each day. In sum, 365 days per year times 4 years times $2 per day adds up to another $2,920. Combine that with the earlier savings, and the total is $4,145 without the interest that would be earned during those 11 years of sixth grade through college. After graduating from college, the successful saver has a job, has an income, and opens an IRA with an initial deposit of $4,000. At 8% average rate of return, that $4,000 will become $128,000 in 45 years. How's that for skipping soft drinks or expensive coffee?"

The students are amazed, fascinated, and convinced. Their life experience now is face-to-face with life possibilities. Of course, they can find a way to save $1 per day now and throughout middle school and high school. They know they can save $2 per day in college. The question becomes, soft drinks and coffee for 11 years or $128,000 at age 68? They need to learn the importance of saving. They need to see how realistic it is to build large amounts of money through a sustained savings program of many small amounts of money. Their past and current life experiences convince them that they can make this happen. Their brains are thinking differently from ever before. Their minds are creating ideas, goals, hopes, plans, dreams, and commitments that surpass their prior visions of the future. Extreme economics has persuaded the students through the power of connecting what they know and what they need to learn. Extreme economics has fascinated the students by connecting their life experience with a new mental picture of what their lives can become. From that moment forward, the classroom is forever energized.

When I initially read the required curriculum for eighth-grade economics 4 years ago, it was immediately obvious that the fundamentals of the curriculum could be expressed in a list of important terms. If students mastered the terms or vocabulary of economics, they could then master the ideas of economics. The teaching challenge to me was to connect these 17 economic vocabulary terms to the life experiences—the wholesome knowledge, interests, and talents—of students. Through these real-life connections, the terms would make sense more easily, more meaningfully, and more relevantly than if students merely memorized the typical glossary or dictionary definitions of the vocabulary terms. The 17 terms follow.

1. Production
2. Distribution
3. Consumption
4. Productivity
5. Technology
6. Competition
7. Specialize
8. Money
9. Scarcity
10. Profit
11. Land, labor, capital
12. Risk
13. Opportunity cost
14. Interdependent
15. Advertisement
16. The law of supply and demand
17. Finances

Throughout 4 years of teaching economics, all classes have thoroughly mastered the 17 core content economic vocabulary terms. Different teaching activities and methods have been used to build on the learning strengths and life experiences of different students. The one class of students who spontaneously yet productively debated which bakery in town made the best doughnuts soon saw a list of 17 applications of the economics terms with a doughnut theme. The example of the term *risk* was "Would people buy a licorice-flavored doughnut—maybe or maybe not." Our concise definition for *risk* was "maybe." The real-life application of risk to the great doughnut debate connected a strong student interest to an important economic idea.

It must be honestly noted that some time was required when I created the 17 doughnut applications to the 17 economic terms. The doughnut debate in class had been spontaneous, had been started when one young scholar commented that a new bakery had just opened in town, and had become a lively discussion in which every student in the class volunteered an opinion about doughnuts or told what his or her favorite doughnut was and where it could be purchased.

No textbook publisher provides the materials I used with my students to apply the 17 economics terms to doughnuts. The textbook publisher provides typical, standard, common supplemental materials. The textbook publisher does not know your students or my students. You know your students. I did not create the doughnut discussion in our class, but when I realized how intrigued the students were about doughnuts and how much learning could be caused by connecting doughnuts to economics, I gladly guided the discussion, and I gladly created materials for us to use the next day to build on this discussion. The economy is lively, dynamic, constantly changing, and always presenting opportunities to people who take the initiative. Teaching economics can be and should be equally lively, dynamic, innovative, and opportunistic.

Doughnuts and economics—you might be skeptical, so let's explore this further. How could the economic terms *production*, *distribution*, and *consumption* be understood in relation to doughnuts? Please think about that and write your thoughts. Now, let's compare our ideas. "A bakery's kitchen is where production of doughnuts happens. The cooks make or produce doughnuts. The doughnut distribution system, how they get from one place to another, can be as simple as carrying trays of doughnuts from the kitchen to the retail-sales part of the bakery, where customers can see the products and purchase products. The distribution system could also include trucks, which are used to deliver bakery products to customers, other retail stores, or other locations of the bakery company."

Consumption means to use a product. Ask eighth graders what the connection between consumption and doughnuts is and you will get one clear answer: "Eat it." The terms *production*, *distribution*, and *consumption* can be understood accurately and vividly in terms of doughnuts. This connects student life experience with the study of economics. This connects the wholesome knowledge, interests, and talents of students with the study of economics. This takes economics out of the limits of a textbook and puts economics into the unlimited imaginations of students. This replaces ordinary, predictable, textbook-chapter-by-chapter, worksheet-by-worksheet economics with extreme economics.

Through the years, students and I have edited the definitions we use for the 17 core content terms. The dictionary or economics textbook glossary could have lengthy, complex, paragraph-length definitions of these terms. College textbooks could have chapters dedicated to one term. A college economics class could spend a semester on economic concepts, applications, implications, and developments related to one of the terms.

The students and I sought concise definitions that accurately and sufficiently conveyed the idea, meaning, and application of the term. This precision enhanced learning. For example, rather than get lost in the maze of words that could define *advertisement* as "any designed and intentional communication effort to inform and persuade consumers about a product, a service, an organization or a cause with the objective or obtaining a favorable action on the part of the consumer," we defined *advertisement* as "commercial." The students have heard and seen many commercials. Their life experience includes hearing and seeing commercials every day. They know the purpose of commercials, so we connect what they know with what they need to learn. Rather than spend time on memorizing a lengthy, wordy, excessive definition of *advertisement*, we make a mental connection with life experience and advertisement, mention some examples, create new advertisements, analyze advertisements, and learn. The goal is to cause learning. Extreme economics causes learning in the most effective and efficient ways, in the most personal and meaningful ways, in the most fascinating and real ways.

Let's revisit the list of 17 core content economics vocabulary terms and include the most recent, "new and improved" concise and precise definitions that eighth graders and I have used (see Table 3.2).

An ever-expanding variety of instructional activities is used to make sure that all students learn, know, can explain, can recall, and can apply these terms. The variety is ever expanding as I learn how current students best learn. I teach to their strengths; to their life experience; to connections between their wholesome knowledge, interests, and talents and what they need to learn now. The following classroom activity is one way students have mastered the terms.

Table 3.2. "New and Improved" Definitions of 17 Core Content Economics Vocabulary Terms

Term	*Meaning*
1. Production	1. To make
2. Distribution	2. To deliver
3. Consumption	3. To use
4. Productivity	4. More with less
5. Technology	5. New, newer, newest
6. Competition	6. Better
7. Specialize	7. One
8. Money	8. What economics is all about
9. Scarcity	9. Not enough
10. Profit	10. To make money
11. Land, labor, capital	11. Earth, work, money
12. Risk	12. Maybe?
13. Opportunity cost	13. A or B, not both
14. Interdependent	14. People and nations working together
15. Advertisement	15. Commercial
16. The law of supply and demand	16. Up, down, determines price; balance; always true
17. Finances	17. Money and prices

technology	*scarcity*	*specialize*	*competition*
productivity	*risk*	*production*	*distribution*
consumption	*advertisement*	*opportunity cost*	*interdependent*
law of supply and demand	*money*	*finances*	*profit*
land	*labor*	*capital*	

Continue the story, which begins below, and use at least 10 words listed above in your part of the story. When you use any of the core content words, underline the word. Using more than 10 words earns you a bonus.

Save, save more, keep saving. Finally, Shawn had saved the money he needed to buy a cell phone. He had cut the yards for several of his neighbors during the summer. He had done some other yard work. He even helped a neighbor with a garage sale, and the neighbor gave him 10% of the total sales.

Half of what he made he put into his saving account to keep it there. The other half of what he made also went into his savings account, but

Shawn and his family knew that he was going to use that half of the money to buy a cell phone and to pay the monthly fees for the cell phone.

This writing task was completed during class in about 8–10 minutes. Some students eagerly read their stories aloud. The cell phone topic instantly connected with the life experience of eighth graders. The writing showed me if any student was having trouble with a term that was used inaccurately. The students took the task seriously, learned independently, and then learned by listening to each other.

The mastery of the core content terms is enhanced with creative homework projects. The students always have a choice from a list of options for homework projects. What they must learn does not vary. How they learn it can, should, and does vary from person to person for many reasons, including different life experiences or different wholesome knowledge, talents, and interests.

Homework projects are given to students one week ahead of the due date. The due date is an exact minute—we remove all doubt by stating the due date and time precisely as the moment class begins on the day the work is due. One week advanced notice gives sufficient time to fit in this work with other demands on the time of each student while not being so much time that students think they can forget it for now and do it later. Each day in class between when the homework project is assigned and when it is due, I check with students individually or collectively to remind them about the homework, to check on their progress, to resolve questions, to hear their ideas about a different way to do the project that they thought would work, and to redundantly emphasize what is due and when it is due.

Here is a homework project assignment, exactly as it was given to students one week before it was due. The same information was on my webpage on the school's website so any student, parent, or guardian could keep up to date.

Due: Friday, March 3, 2006, 9:37 a.m. EST

Note: There is no "I don't have it" or "It's at home."

Take the 17 core content terms—see list below—and do one of the following. Everything will be G-rated, legal, and ethical.

1. Create a card game that uses all of the terms. There would be at least 34 cards in the deck that you make so each term and its definition

will be used at least once. Write a two- to three-paragraph explanation of how the card game is played. Name the game.

2. Create a collage that shows, through words and pictures, each of the core content terms and (a) what they mean or (b) an example of them in use.

3. Create a vocabulary picture minibook—maybe similar to those old books you read years ago to learn the alphabet, with "A" on one page and words that begin with "A" pictured—using all of the core content terms. The book would be at least 19 pages long so you have a front cover, a back cover, and at least one page per term. Idea: Take five sheets of paper, fold them like pages in a book, and you have 20 pages.

4. You are the host of a radio talk show called "Save, Save More, Keep Saving." Write the script of the talk show, with callers calling you and your conversation with them. Use all of the 17 core content terms so their meaning is clear, or use the 17 terms and include their meaning. Underline each term whenever you use it.

5. Make a set of 17 flash cards. On one side is the core content term. On the other side is (a) the definition of the word and (b) a drawing you make or a cut/paste picture showing the meaning of the word or an application/example of the word.

Terms:

law of supply and demand	land, labor, capital	advertisement	finances
production	distribution	consumption	productivity
technology	competition	specialize	money
scarcity	profit	opportunity cost	risk
interdependent			

The brain can manage several thoughts at once, so I look for ways to teach more than economics within the teaching of economics whenever multithinking opportunities arise. When I grade a writing task such as the cell phone story or when I grade homework projects such as the one about the 17 vocabulary terms, I keep a list of words that students misspelled. I then create an economics activity that includes the misspelled words in their misspelled form exactly as the students originally wrote the words. The students' responses to a teacher-provided paper with misspelled words ranges from laughter to shock, from being concerned about seeing their misspellings on the page to being—or acting—offended that their teacher would perpetrate misspellings on them.

The following story was written for my students after I compiled a list of words they misspelled. The story has many ideas that relate to economics and address the spelling skills of students. This increases our productivity, which is, of course, an important economic term and concept. This is another way that the extreme economics approach enables students to learn economics by experiencing economics.

too	*favorite*	*probably*	*breakfast*	*replace*	*consumed*
different	*tasting*	*clothes*	*processed*	*protein*	*scent*
business	*apparent*	*replacing*	*label*	*commercial*	*delicious*

Chocolate is probly your favrite flavor of ice cream, but you might like other flavors, to. Have you ever wanted to have lots of chocolate for breckfast, but you had to replase your chocolate cravings with hunger for healthy food that had vitamins, protien, and was not as delicous taseing as chocolate? Read the lable of our new breckfast food and it will be aparent that we are in the busness of replasing that healthy, but bad taseing food with just what you have always wanted: the sent of chocolate, the flavor of chocolate, the nutrition of new, healthy chocolate in every bite that is consumpted. This is a difrent breckfast experience which will have you jumping out of bed, putting on your school close fast so you can get to breckfast immediately. Our new cereal is called, Chocolate Fitness. Maybe you have seen our comercial which shows rivers of chocolate sauce flowing into fields of wheat and procesed together into bountiful bowls of Chocolate Fitness cereal. So, call 1-555-FITNESS and request a free box of great tasting, super healthy Chocolate Fitness Cereal.

The case study method has been used quite effectively in college and graduate school economics classes. As students analyze, evaluate, assess, and explore the facts, the details, the decisions, the issues, the mistakes, and the successes within one real business situation, that case becomes part of the knowledge those students can take with them when they encounter similar situations in their business careers.

During an eighth-grade economics class discussion about businesses, a student commented that one of our topics reminded him of the lemonade stand business he had organized when he was younger. That was a perfect opportunity for extreme economics to connect with the life experiences of students. We heard his description of the lemonade stand, the difficulties and successes, and managing the business. I asked him if it was agreeable for me to use his entrepreneurial experience as the basis of a case study story I would write for our class. He was delighted with the idea, so I wrote the following case study. Please note that this item originally appeared in *Extreme Learning* (2004). Note also that, as the economic terms are applied, the meanings become more sophisticated to help develop the students' reasoning, thinking, and application skills (terms are included at the end of the story, each designated with a letter).

CHAD'S LEMONADE STAND, PART I

"It's so hot today and there's nothing to do. It was hot yesterday and there was nothing to do. I've read every book I bought at the book fair. I've been to the pool enough to last forever. I'm broke so I can't go to the movies. Now what?" Chad soon realized that being broke would inspire an endeavor that could fill his time with something worth doing and fill his pockets with extra money.

Chad was advised to set up a lemonade stand on the sidewalk in the front yard, close but not too close to the street. People who walk by might want to buy lemonade on this very hot July day. This location is an example of using (a); doing the work to start the business is an example of (b). People who drive by might be interested, too. It was worth a try, and there really was nothing else to do. How many times can you watch reruns of old situation comedies? Another day of indoor, boring television programs from the 1970s made the lemonade stand idea sound even better.

Chad thought to himself, *Okay, what do I need to get this business started? I need lemonade, cups, ice, a pitcher, probably a sign, a box for money, and—oops—money. I don't have any money.* In economics, money used to start and continue a business is called (c). "How can I start this business if I don't have any money? This business is going to fail before it ever starts if I can't get the supplies. Now what can I do?" This is an example of (d): No one person or country has or can make all it needs or wants.

Chad has a (e) of money, which means not enough; his demand for it is greater than his supply of it. If he could convince someone that the lemonade stand would make a (f) (make money, as total revenue would be greater than total costs), perhaps that person would invest in this idea. Chad has the land, and he is willing to do the labor, but he needs the capital, or money. Fortunately, his parents were willing to invest in his business, but they told him, "The money we invest in your lemonade stand is money we cannot give you to go to the movies. Having the lemonade stand means not using the money to go to the movies." This is an example of (g): Doing A means you cannot do B. Chad agreed to the deal. He would take the $12 to buy his first order of supplies—lemonade mix, cups, sugar, and ice; he would borrow pitchers and an ice cooler from his family, so he did not have to buy those. He would get water from the kitchen and that would not cost him anything.

Chad had to ask himself some questions about (h): Would anyone buy his lemonade? Maybe, maybe not. Further, would he sell enough of it to cover the $12 in costs and, he hoped, have some money left over as (i)? He figured that, with the supplies he had, he could make 72 cups of lemonade. He would charge 25 cents per cup, and that would bring in (j). So his profit would be (k). He could pay back $6 of the $12 he borrowed. If he could use the other part of that income, $12 of the $18, to sell another 72 cups, his new profit would again be (l) and he could get out of debt; plus, he would have $12 and he could buy another round of supplies, or he could just declare victory.

So, he was almost ready to open his lemonade stand. Chad was convinced that the plan would work, but he thought he needed some (m) (a commercial intended to sell a product or service). He decided to make a big sign using some materials he had at home. *Lemonade 25 cents!!* He was confident about his (n) (what is used to buy products or services) and his (o) (how much money is needed to buy a particular product or service). Business conditions looked good—the weather was hot, the lemonade was cold, the advertising sign was big, the price was fair, and the risk seemed low. He had a good (p) (how much is available) of lemonade and knew there was good (q) (how much people wanted the product). He knew there was some (r) (Will anyone buy the lemonade? Can he make a profit?), but he was hopeful. Plus he was the only person in his neighborhood setting up a lemonade stand today, so there was no direct (s) (better) except for the convenience store nearby, but Chad's price was better than its, so he was ready to go into business. He had completed (t) of the lemonade (making it), he had completed the (u) of the lemonade (getting it to the customers), and now was the time for consumers to begin (v) of the lemonade (purchasing it and using it).

The first customer walked up. "Hey, Chad. What's this all about?"

Chad replied, "It's only 25 cents for a cup of lemonade. How about being my first customer?" Chad hoped for a quick sale and that this customer would tell other people.

"Well, maybe a free sample first and then, if I like it, I'll buy some."

Chad thought to himself. *Free sample. That's not part of the plan. I'd have to give that away and get nothing for it. Can I afford that? Can I still make a profit if I give it away? If I give away 36 free samples and sold 36 cups, I would lose money. I can't do it.*

"Free sample, huh? I can't really do that, but here's what I can do. You try it, and if you don't like it I'll give you your money back."

"Okay." Trevor tried it and had to admit that it was good. Trevor wondered if he would drink it and say it was no good to avoid paying, but by drinking it, he showed it was good. Plus he did not want to cheat Chad since they were friends. "Hey, Chad, that's really good. I've been at the park playing baseball, and the concession stand there charges 50 cents for lemonade. You should make a lot of money. See ya."

So during the next half hour or so, people stopped to buy or talk or to just see what was going on. One person asked Chad if he had any coffee or soft drinks. "No, I just have lemonade." Chad had decided to (w) (make or sell one product or service).

After about 45 to 60 minutes, Chad had sold all his lemonade. All of it. He realized why it sold so fast. There had been a big baseball tournament at the park, and when it was over, a lot of people drove by or walked by Chad's lemonade stand. He had picked the right location and the right time. He wondered how he could improve his (x) (make more lemonade with less time spent making it) so he would never run out. He had just run out and there were three people who wanted to buy. He would have to go back to the store to get more supplies, and then he would have to make the lemonade; the customers could not wait. Maybe there was some new (y) (new, newer, newest improvement in efficiency, cost, time, or quality due to change) in doing this that would help him to never run out.

The results were good: 72 cups sold at 25 cents each means that total revenue was (z). When Chad counted the money, he realized that he was short 25 cents. How did that happen? Oh yeah, he did give one free sample. A lady with a van full of baseball players stopped. Chad figured that one free sample that might lead to eight sales was worth it. To get out of the debt right away, Chad paid back the $12 he borrowed, plus 75 cents of the profit. Hey, the person who invested the capital deserves some of the profit, right? That left Chad with (aa). Should that be put into another business, should it be saved, or should it be spent on going to the movies? Should he expand his business? Does he need a business partner?

CHAD'S LEMONADE STAND: WORD BANK/ANSWER KEY

a. land
b. labor
c. capital
d. interdependence
e. scarcity
f. profit
g. opportunity cost
h. risk
i. profit
j. $18
k. $6
l. $6
m. advertising
n. money/finances
o. price
p. supply
q. demand
r. risk
s. competition
t. production
u. distribution
v. consumption

w. specialize
x. productivity
y. technology
z. $18
aa. $5

CHAD'S LEMONADE STAND, PART II

1. Using words and drawings, please describe and show a traditional neighborhood lemonade stand.
2. Using words and drawings, please describe and show a 21st-century high-tech neighborhood lemonade stand.
3. List the similarities in the two lemonade stands and the differences between the two lemonade stands.
4. If you opened a lemonade stand, what is the one action you could take that would impress customers so your lemonade stand would become more successful than any other lemonade stand?

CHAD'S LEMONADE STAND, PART III

Competition by any other name is still competition. The essence of competition is doing something better. Better could be measured in price, in quality of the product, in service, in innovation/uniqueness, or in value. Other ways for products to improve could include the following.

Let's return to the story of Chad's lemonade stand. A profit has been made and Chad decides to continue his business. His investors were pleased that their investment earned a healthy dividend for them. They were glad to invest again in Chad's growing business. Chad had asked customers what they liked best about his lemonade and what else they would like from a lemonade stand.

The survey results were clear. People liked the taste of the lemonade, people liked the value, people thought the price was fair, and people thought they had been treated politely. There were some suggestions for improvement: Have more than one size of serving; have pink lemonade and regular lemonade; since it is summer, sell ice cream also.

Well, Chad opened his lemonade stand the next day. He still had the original 8-ounce cup of lemonade for 25 cents, plus he had a 12-ounce cup for 35 cents. He also had a special offer: 3 of the 12-ounce cups for $1. The day was hot and sunny. Business was good. Then the unexpected happened. Across the street, another lemonade stand opened, but this lemonade stand was different. People could get soft drinks here in addition to lemonade. People could get ice cream. People could get homemade cookies.

It was obvious that some of Chad's customers were now going to the new Lemonade Plus stand across the street.

What should Chad do now?

1.
2.
3.
4.

As Chad makes some changes, what would you as the owner/manager of the new Lemonade Plus stand do?

1.
2.
3.
4.

One benefit of using the extreme economics teaching approach is that the teacher can sometimes follow the students to the destination the teacher established. The case study of Chad's lemonade stand was created when I followed a student's comment about his childhood experience as a lemonade stand owner/operator. Using the case study, I followed the student's idea to my original destination of students' mastering and applying the essential vocabulary of economics. The teacher's destination for the students was their learning. The path that most effectively took us to that learning was a path one student suggested that we take. This extreme adventure of blazing new learning paths to reach established curriculum destinations enables the teacher to learn how current students learn while causing current students to learn.

Parts II and III of the lemonade stand case study were genuine extensions that grew from the profound classroom discussion we had about part I. The students' questions, ideas, answers, and input were followed, applied, and incorporated Socratically by the teacher to get the students to the desired destination. Everyone wins this way.

My students are taught that economics is all about money but that life is about much more than money. Life is about family, friends, what you believe in, what you are dedicated to, goals you set and pursue, accomplishments, helping people, and the honorable standards you live by. The students are taught how to manage money; they are not taught to be obsessed with money. The students realize that if the money parts of life are managed well, the other parts of life can go much better than if money problems happened. The students realize that the money mistakes that people make are usually unnecessary and are often self-inflicted. As they reflect on their life experiences with money, they acknowledge that wiser decisions could have been made in some financial matters. Many of these wiser decisions were in the day-to-day ordinary financial transactions, where the amount of money involved in each transaction is small; but a small amount of money wasted day after day will add up to a large amount of money after a month, a year, or a few years. Had that money been managed wisely, with some of it saved each month, the total savings could have been substantial.

Elementary school students, middle school students, and high school students are experts on soft drinks, so soft drinks can be an easy connection with economics and student life experiences. Checking newspaper advertisements for prices and noticing prices in local stores can provide data for economics math calculations that students will find interesting and surprising. Consider the following information as a starting point for discussion about economics at the level of day-to-day student life experience.

Price and price per ounce: Price divided by ounces = price per ounce
Soft drink:

a. 2 liters (67.6 ounces)
   @ 99 cents = 1.46 cents per ounce
   @ $1.19 = 1.76 cents per ounce

b. 6 bottles, 24 ounces per bottle
   @ $2.50 = 1.74 cents per ounce
   @ $2.88 = 2.00 cents per ounce
c. 12 cans, 12 ounces each
   @ 3 for $8 = 1.85 cents per ounce
   @ $2.99 = 2.08 cents per ounce
d. 24 cans, 12 ounces each
   @ $4.99 = 1.73 cents per ounce
   @ $5.99 = 2.08 cents per ounce

What questions could you ask students based on these competing prices on various sizes of soft drink containers? Please think of five questions.

1.
2.
3.
4.
5.

Let's add this question: A family usually buys two 24-can packages of soft drinks per week. They pay $5.99 plus 6% sales tax for each package. Including tax, each package costs $6.35, so each week they spend $12.70 on soft drinks. How much do they spend on soft drinks in 1 year?

The students do the math of 52 times $12.70 and get the answer of $660.40 and then hear the question "How could the family save some or all of that money in wise, legal, ethical ways?"

The discussion will include ideas such as the following: use coupons, watch for super sale prices, buy only one package per week, substitute powder-mix beverage options, do not buy soft drinks, and work for a soft drink company to get free products.

We then do the math a step further. If the family avoids the $660.40 cost for 18 years, how much is saved? The answer is $11,887.20, which does not include interest that would be earned during those 18 years. I then ask the students what educational cost could that money help pay for when a person is 18 years old. College. A moment of productive and contemplative silence passes as students realize that one part of a plan that helps pay for college is to eliminate the $12.70 per week spent by a family for soft drinks. Opportunity cost—A or B, not both—at this point is not an economic theory or distant concept; it is a personal and practical reality.

Student life experience is a powerful classroom resource. Student life experiences can connect with what students need to learn. When the classroom is a place of continual connections between the wholesome knowledge, interests, and talents of students and what they need to learn, the results can be productive. Because of the connections with the real lives of students, there are no wasted minutes on "Why do we have to learn this?" or "When will we ever need to know this?" There is no search for ways to motivate students, because the curriculum is being connected to parts of real life that the students are already motivated about.

In the next chapter, we will probe further and deeper into the possibilities of students achieving mastery of the economics curriculum through being immersed in extreme economics.

4

HOW TO FULLY APPLY STUDENT LIFE EXPERIENCE TO ACHIEVE MASTERY

Students are often aware of businesses. They go with a parent or guardian to run errands at various stores, shops, shopping centers, and malls. They see and hear advertisements for businesses. They notice a new store that is under construction. They go to a neighborhood restaurant that has been owned and operated by a local family for two generations.

Students may not know about all or about some of the work that must occur for businesses to open initially and to remain open in the long term. To increase awareness of, to build knowledge of, and to attain mastery of economics, case studies can be used.

The first case study in this chapter was written for one class I taught. It includes many interests of students, from products I hear them mention to career goals they told me they have set. The case study was designed with one group of students in mind, so it was uniquely created for them; however, ideas in this case study could inspire new case studies or could be modified. As you read this, please think of connections that are being made between the life experiences of students and the economics curriculum. Notice also that the case study sequence builds on each episode as the business owner experiences many steps in the entrepreneurial process.

CASE STUDY I

For years, you have dreamed of and seriously thought about opening your own business. Your career has been quite successful, but you still hope to apply your entrepreneurial energies and talents as the owner of a business. Cooking has been a hobby of yours for many years. Your family and friends have always told you that you are a great cook. Your cookies, cakes, pies, and other homemade baked delicacies are always eaten quickly at any meal at home and at social events when you bring them.

Also, you have taught yourself a lot about computers. You can take them apart and put them together. You have learned how to write rather sophisticated software, and you can operate any technology system to maximize the results. Another hobby of yours is photography, and you can do anything with digital cameras and computers. You sometimes make one-of-a-kind books as presents for children. These unique, personalized books combine photographs you take and stories you write.

Your goal is still to get promoted to be CIO (chief information officer) of the company you work for, but that has not happened yet. So, you have wondered how your cooking talents, your other hobbies, and your technology expertise could all be combined in a way that would make you your own boss. You have friends who are lawyers, doctors, political leaders, retired military officers, police officers, and veterinarians, and some of them have said occasionally that if you ever start a business, they would be interested in investing in it, so that is a possibility.

A friend who is an orthodontist made this suggestion: "Why not combine many of your skills? Open a restaurant and arts/crafts activity place combination. Fill it with computers and cameras that people can use. Maybe you could include cooking classes, especially with all of these baked treats you know how to cook. You could have some food that is served fast and some that is fancier. You could have all kinds of coffee and tea but also snacks and treats that children and teenagers would like. Make it a comfortable place where people stay, eat, talk, read, and work and come back day after day. If you have all kinds of computers and Internet access, some people might use your place as their branch office. You might even include a conference room, and people could have meetings there or have clubs that gather there. It could even be a place for birthday parties with video connections to friends and family members who are out of town. And be sure to include your homemade doughnuts on the menu. I never knew how you made those, but they are better than anything at any bakery."

You consider the idea. It would take a lot of money to start this new business. You need a location that is convenient and has a lot of traffic going in front of it. You need all of the equipment. If you build a custom-designed building, that will be expensive. If you rent a place, that will cost a lot, too. You will need employees. You will need to advertise. You will need to budget and spend a lot of money to start the business before you get any money coming in from sales. Is this idea worth the risk?

Yes, it is worth the risk because

1.
2.
3.
4.

No, it is not worth the risk because

1.
2.
3.
4.

Okay. You decide that this new business is worth the risk, but you also decide that you need to have a business partner or two. You would like for them to invest money, and you hope that at least one of your business partners will help manage and operate the business. What reasons would you use to convince one or two people to become business partners with you in this new endeavor?

1.
2.
3.
4.

Okay. One partner agrees to invest 20% of the money you will need to open the business. Another partner agrees to invest 10% of the money you will need to open the business. You have savings that will provide 10% of the money you need, and you intend to work full-time at the new business. One of your partners—the one providing 10% of the money—has agreed to be there 20 hours each week, but she is going to keep her full-time job as a writer for a local advertising agency and some local monthly neighborhood newspapers. The other partner is an attorney and cannot provide any work hours but will visit as often as possible and provide legal advice. The other 60% of the money you need will have to come from a bank.

What questions do you expect the bank officials to ask you before they decide on your loan request?

1.
2.
3.
4.
5.

The bank asks for details of your business plan. This would include the finances in detail, so list every expense you can think of that will be required for you to open this new business:

1.
2.
3.
4.
5.

Wait. What are we going to call this new business? A great name would be

1.
2.
3.
4.

The bank agrees to support your project, but it will provide only 50% of what you need. How will you get the other 10% that is still needed?

1.
2.
3.
4.

Okay, you get another business partner, who agrees to invest the other 10% of the money you need. Now, it is time to begin the actual work that will take you from the idea you have now to a new business opening in 10 weeks from today. You have found a location to rent the space you need. You think it is a good location. The location is on New Center Road in the Bluegrass Shopping Center. What will need to be done during the next 10 weeks?

Time	What must be done
10 weeks to go	
9 weeks to go	
8 weeks to go	
7 weeks to go	
6 weeks to go	
5 weeks to go	
4 weeks to go	
3 weeks to go	
2 weeks to go	
1 week to go	
Grand opening day	

P.S. What is the name of your new business?

Oops. On the day your business is scheduled to open, our area has severe thunderstorms during much of the day. People are not very eager to get out in the weather. You and your partners and all but one of your employees get to the shop, but there are very few customers. What do you do?

Three months later a new business similar to yours opens across the street. This is a food court with six fast-food places, plus an arcade, a

Starbucks, an Apple Computer store, and a NASCAR store. What do you do to compete successfully, legally, and ethically with G-rated actions?

After 6 months, you think about opening a second location. There is a place available in the Boyle Park area, but the rent is quite expensive. There is also space available in a new building downtown. What are reasons for and against opening a second location?

For	Against
1.	1.
2.	2.
3.	3.
4.	4.

It is 8 months since you opened your shop, and your business is doing well. That new "food court plus" that competes with your business has taken some of your business, but both shops seem to be successful. In the past two months, you have been concerned that some of your customers who used to come in daily or almost every day have come in less often. When you asked some of them why, they said, "Well, you know, your place was new and unique at first, but now it just seems to be ordinary. Maybe you could add something new." Good point. Businesses constantly need to listen to customers and keep up with what customers want or need. What changes and improvements would you make to your business as part of the first anniversary party you have at your business location? Think of one action you could take in each of the following areas:

Menu:
Special deals:
Advertising:
Frequent-customer reward program:
Promotional event:
Other:

After being in business for 14 months, you are given an offer from a local entrepreneur, who would like to buy your business. The offer is reasonable; in fact, it is very attractive. What reasons are there to accept this offer? What reasons are there to reject the offer?

Accept	Reject
1.	1.
2.	2.
3.	3.
4.	4.

The 17 core content terms and applications to Case Study 1 are listed in Table 4.1. On the column at the right, explain how each core content term is applied in Case Study 1.

That case study and other case studies can serve many purposes—namely, the students begin to realize

1. the complexity of taking a business idea into the marketplace,
2. how to apply economic vocabulary terms to a real-life setting,
3. the variety of skills needed to make a business succeed, and
4. a depth of thought that must be sustained over time.

Table 4.1. The 17 Core Content Terms and Applications to Case Study 1

Term	*Application to Case Study*
1. The law of supply and demand	
2. Production	
3. Distribution	
4. Consumption	
5. Productivity	
6. Technology	
7. Competition	
8. Specialize	
9. Money	
10. Scarcity	
11. Profit	
12. Land, labor, capital	
13. Risk	
14. Opportunity cost	
15. Interdependent	
16. Advertisement	
17. Finances	

This case study has multiple aspects, many questions, some analysis, critical thinking, sequential reasoning, analytical reading, and justification for decisions. What other benefits could students gain from this case study?

The case study about a new business may give some students a taste of entrepreneurial activity, which builds a hunger for more. By the time students are in middle school, their life experience may already include some entrepreneurial efforts that they did not realize were so economically sophisticated.

Children and teenagers sometimes make trades: one baseball card for two baseball cards, two cookies for one brownie. "You do my chores at home for me today, and I will do your chores for the next two days." These trades are similar to bartering, an exchange method still used today in some places but more commonly used in earlier historical times. Doing an economics activity about bartering could academically connect with a world history class discussion of weekly, monthly, seasonal, or annual events in some cultures, when the village became or becomes an open-air market, where bartering is the only, the preferred, or the optional method of exchange.

The following bartering activity begins with each student getting a sheet that resembles Table 4.2. One commodity would be highlighted, and that is the item you bring to the village marketplace. You will barter to eventually have two items from each category (a, b, and c). For example, if you begin with 40 chickens, you could barter some chickens to

Table 4.2. Bartering Activity

Began With	*Ended With*
a. 40 chickens	
a. 20 cows	
a. 10 horses	
a. 40 pigs	
b. 50 baskets of apples	
b. 50 bushels of corn	
b. 50 bushels of wheat	
b. 30 pails of milk	
c. 15 sewn cloth coats	
c. 15 pairs of shoes	
c. 30 blankets	

get 1 cow, 1 basket of apples, 1 pail of milk, 1 coat, and 1 blanket, thus giving you two items from each of the three categories.

Students may ask, "How do we know who wins?" A teacher could reply, "If everyone in the community gets everything he or she needs, we have many winners, including each person individually and all people together." A teacher might say, "The person who ends with the highest percentage of the commodity they began with is the one who wins. If you start with 40 chickens and barter away 6 chickens to get your other products, you kept 85% of your chickens; however, do you need all of those chickens? If not, maybe you need to barter away all of your chickens to get the victory you need." There are many ways to determine winners in an economy, because needs, wants, and goals vary from person to person.

As a student barters 1 chicken for 1 pig, the student changes the number of chickens from 40 to 39 and in the Ended With column puts 1 across from pigs. When all bartering is done, the Ended With column shows the results.

The bartering is done person to person, so after confirming that all students understand the process, the rules, and the objective, the students need to begin talking to each other. Moving around the room will be necessary so that each participant can talk with each potential deal maker. Remind the students of your classroom rules about noise, cooperation, and movement.

What questions could you ask the students after the bartering activity to maximize their learning from analysis of, understanding of, and application of the activity?

1.
2.
3.
4.
5.
6.
7.
8.

What observations and conclusions would you expect from students as they present their ideas of the bartering experience?

1.
2.
3.
4.
5.
6.
7.
8.

What connections could you point out or have students point out between their life experiences and bartering? How could they benefit from bartering now and in the future?

Before going further, it will be beneficial to evaluate the case study activity and the bartering activity in terms of their effectiveness to teach students the essential lessons about economics that the respondents to the research survey said were vital.

The research clearly emphasized that children and teenagers need to save, save more, keep saving. The students need to realize the immediate and long-term advantages of savings, know how to save money, and make saving a high priority. How does Save. Save more. Keep saving. apply to the case study? The entrepreneur had saved money, as had other investors, which they were willing to provide for part of the financing of the new business.

The research strongly advised that credit is deceptive and potentially destructive. The bartering activity allowed no credit. Five chickens for one pig, maybe. Five chickens for a pig next week, no.

The entrepreneur did borrow some money from the bank, and other investors provided some funds. That is common with new businesses and is a direct example of the research advice to do the math of money. The math convinced the bank that a loan for this new business was a reasonable risk.

Let's edit the 10 findings from the research to simplify the thoughts that you will add to the following chart (see Table 4.3). The detailed statements of the survey results are in Chapter 1. For our purposes in Chapter 4, the abbreviated and edited list of research findings will work. For each research conclusion listed in the table, please think of how that conclusion can be taught through the case study and the bartering activity. Fear not, in this book many more examples of extreme economics

Table 4.3. Research Findings and Additional Thoughts

Research Findings	*How the Case Study Helps Students Learn This*	*How Bartering Helps Students Learn This*
1. Save		
2. Save now; habit of saving		
3. Money plan; budget		
4. Credit is deceptive		
5. Spend less than you make		
6. Life is more than money		
7. Math measures economics		
8. Maximize your education		
9. Work ethic		
10. People are more important than money		

teaching will be presented. If you conclude that many, but not most, of the research conclusions can be taught through these two activities, that is fine. The other activities included will provide ample ways to teach the skills and knowledge listed in the survey findings while also enabling a teacher to confirm that students learned the school's, the school district's, and the state's economic curriculum.

The next set of extreme economics activities emphasize the research finding that the measurement system of economics is math. Many of the following questions will teach as much math as economics so that teachers get that efficiency and students get to see that subjects at school can complement one another rather than exist in pure isolation.

Some of these questions and problems could be used as a thought starter to begin class and warm up the brains. Some of these could be used together to build a depth of knowledge, as one idea expands another idea. Better yet, teachers can modify these problems so that the new problems more precisely connect with the life experiences and the wholesome knowledge, interests, and talents of students.

1. You have $500 in a checking account. Write three checks so that there is $100 left in the account:
   Who the check is made out to? Amount of check?
   a.
   b.
   c.
   Total of the three checks: ____________________

2. A store charges the following prices for a 2-liter bottle of a soft drink during a 4-week period:
   Week 1 = $1.49
   Week 2 = $1.19
   Week 3 = 99 cents
   Week 4 = 79 cents
   - What would you expect to happen to sales of 2-liter bottles of the soft drink as this 4-week period goes from Week 1 to Week 2 to Week 3 to Week 4?
   - Why do you think that will happen?
   - What would you expect to happen to the store's total profit from 2-liter bottles of the soft drink as this 4-week period goes from Week 1 to Week 2 to Week 3 to Week 4?
   - Why do you think that will happen?
   - Which price do you think will work best for the store?
   - Give two reasons why you think that will be the best price for the store to charge:

     a.

     b.
3. Facts: The house costs $88,900, but your offer of $85,000 is accepted by the owner. You check with some banks and find various interest rates. Compare and contrast these mortgage plans for principal (amount borrowed) and interest (cost of the money). Note: Insurance would cost about $300 per year; property taxes would be about $700 per year.

Down payment	$5,000	$5,000	$5,000
Amount of mortgage	$80,000	$80,000	$80,000
Interest rate	6.5%	8.0%	6.25%
Length in years of mortgage	30	30	15
Monthly payment	$506.40	$587.20	$686.40
Payment total in 1 year	_____	_____	_____
Payment total for life of the loan	_____	_____	_____

Conclusions:

4. Two large pizzas for $16, or three medium pizzas for $16, or five small pizzas for $16—which is the best deal? Each large pizza has a diameter of 16 inches. Each medium pizza has a diameter of 12 inches. Each small pizza has a diameter of 10 inches.

Reflect: No writing, just think about it
Evaluate: What is known? What needs to be known?
Act: What process can be used to find the answer?
Okay. Let's do the math of the three pizza deals.
Learn: What conclusions can be reached? How can those conclusions be applied?
Would the answer be any different if the three medium pizzas cost $15.50 and the five small pizzas cost $15.00?

5. A grocery store offers 1 liter of bottled water for 50 cents each if you also buy $10 worth of other groceries. Another store sells 1 liter of bottled water for 99 cents each, and no additional purchase is needed. A third store sells 1 liter of bottled water for $1.10 each and will double the value of any coupon you use. You need to buy some water in 1-liter bottles, but what other factors should be considered in deciding which store should be selected? Could it make sense to go to more than one store? For what reasons?
6. In consideration of other products—such as bottled water, salt, cereal—what does the word supply mean?
7. In consideration of products—such as bottled water, salt, cereal—what does demand mean?
8. As far as prices are concerned, when there is a large supply of something and there is no demand for that product, what happens to the price if the people who have the product really want to get it sold?
9. Explain why the price change you stated in Question 8 would happen.
10. Think of four different brands of cereal—real brands or four you make up. List them and tell what would be the strongest reason you could give in a commercial for each cereal, to convince people that they should buy that cereal. An example is given for you, so do not use that cereal as one of your four. Use four different reasons, one unique reason for each of the four cereals.

Brand of cereal	Reason people should buy it
a. Oatmeal	a. It is very healthy for you.
b.	b.
c.	c.
d.	d.
e.	e.

11. Using two or three sentences with strong reasons to explain your thinking, whether you agree or disagree with the following statement: "When a person buys a car, the most important fact to consider in the decision of what car to buy is the price."
12. Explain what the phrase buy and hold means to people who are interested in having shares of stock.
13. A new coffee shop sold $1,000,000 worth of coffee in 1 year. The next year, its sales increased 20% and it added three varieties of hot chocolate. Hot chocolate accounted for 5% of the store's total sales in the second year the store was open. How much sales did they have of hot chocolate?

Now, continue creating economics thought starters to begin a class with or complete lessons that build on the math of economics. A shopping trip to the grocery store can become the basis of an extreme economics lesson. Sales receipts can be saved and used in an extreme economics lesson. Frequently getting input from students about their recent experiences that connect with economics can be the basis for classroom activities that cause students to learn the economics curriculum and the economics rules and skills from the survey research done for this book.

Most children and teenagers are interested in music. They have their favorite singers. They dream of attending a concert and perhaps actually get to attend a concert of a popular musician. They hear music as the soundtrack of a movie. They play a musical instrument. They are in the school band, orchestra, or chorus. They help with music at their church. They went to a music camp in the summer.

The next extreme economics lesson connects economics with music. The lesson has several parts that flow logically and serve unique purposes yet fit together for comprehensive conclusions.

Maximizing profit: The symbiosis of capitalism—how customers and businesses can benefit together
First: Records, eight-track tapes, cassette tapes, or compact discs

- What is similar about those four forms of music playing?
- What is different about those four forms of music playing?

Second: If a store wanted to maximize its profit from selling compact discs, the store manager could test several different prices. Do the math, please.

Compact disc price to customer	Compact disc cost to store	Profit of each compact disc	No. of compact discs sold	Total profit
$14.99	$8.99	$6.00	40	$240.00
13.99	8.99		50	
12.99	8.99		60	
11.99	7.99		75	
10.99	7.99		80	
9.99	6.99		120	
8.99	6.99		130	

- What price to consumers maximized the profit to the business?
- What reason could there be to charge a lower price to consumers?
- Why did the store's cost per compact disc drop when it bought more from the compact disc production/distribution system?

Third: As popular as the pocket-size music players that use songs downloaded via computer are, what will replace these pocket-size music machines, just as records were replaced by tapes or compact discs? Invent that new system.

- What does it do?
- How does it do it?
- What would convince consumers to buy it even after they bought and liked their pocket-size system?
- What's the name of the new music-playing system you created?

Fourth: Think of the overall topic of music-playing systems, prices of compact discs, and a new music-playing system. How does all of that relate to economic terms such as the following:

a. Supply and demand
b. Technology
c. Competition
d. Opportunity cost
e. Profit
f. Money

g. Advertisement
h. Scarcity

It must be noted that what will make these economics lessons work and other equally extreme economics lessons work is the interaction between students and the teacher. The materials and the lessons shared in this book are intended to show how economics can be taught through application of and connection with the life experiences of students, plus the wholesome knowledge, interests, and talents of students and the economics curriculum, vocabulary, rules, or skills to be mastered.

Use the examples, lessons, activities, and materials in this book as starting points for your creative thinking about how to teach economics. The ideas in this book have worked well with my students because they connected with their real lives; their real-life experiences; and their wholesome knowledge, interests, and talents. I change how I teach with each class of students so that I can tap into their uniqueness as individuals and as a group. That gives me the forever amazing, challenging, and energizing experience of learning how my current students best learn. I know that they will respond to the extreme economics approach in general, but I get to discover and then create the exact activities that will cause the best learning. Learning about how students learn is a treasured ongoing life experience of mine that enables me to provide the most effective and most extreme learning experiences for students. Extreme economics is as much an idea, a way of thinking about teaching economics, as it is the precise classroom instructional activities that will implement that idea, that way of thinking, so learning is caused in the brain, in the mind, in the life of every student.

The seasons of a school year continually renew and expand the life experience resources that students bring to the extreme economics classroom and that teachers can use to cause learning of and mastery of economics.

Students may have noticed the many back-to-school sales, commercials, promotions, and marketing events at businesses in the weeks before the school year began. A teacher could collect a large supply of brochures, coupons, advertisements, and offers from these sales to use in class as examples of competition, finances, opportunity cost, risk, profit, money production, distribution, consumption, supply, and demand.

The tempting offers in some of the back-to-school sales could also be used by a teacher to introduce the personal economic insights from the survey research. How does a family save, save more, keep saving in the midst of back-to-school advertisements encouraging people to spend, spend more, keep spending? How could a back-to-school budget help a student and a family manage money wisely?

What connections could be made between the back-to-school shopping season and the research findings and advice that credit is deceptive and that it is wise to live within your means?

The economic system in this country and the continually new life experiences of students combine to provide new teaching resources throughout the school year. Soon after the back-to-school events in stores, students may notice or hear about Labor Day furniture sales, model closeout car sales, new fashions for the fall or winter seasons, early-start sales for Thanksgiving family events, very-early-start sales for Christmas gifts followed by more generous discounts right after Christmas.

Activities that students are involved with during the school year provide new topics for extreme economics discussions and activities. What is the financial impact on the athletic budget of a high school when an unusually large crowd attends a football game? What costs are associated with new uniforms for the marching band and with getting that band to all of the band competition events during marching season?

What is the economic reasoning behind a middle school or an elementary school reducing the number of soft drink options in vending machines and increasing the number of juice and water options? What is the economic impact of that change?

When an elementary school student tells her teacher that her older sister just got her driving license but has to pay for something called "car insurance," what economic lesson or math calculation could that inspire?

When an elementary school student comes in on Monday talking about going to see a movie over the weekend and says, "But the popcorn and candy cost so much that we did not get any of that. Instead, we used a coupon to get a free soft drink," what economic connections can be made? What interdisciplinary possibilities emerge, such as writing a polite letter to the movie theater manager asking about the high prices for snacks? Could a language arts class make that a productive activity that applies student life experience?

Middle school or high school students may discuss making money by shoveling snow on a day when a winter storm canceled school. What extreme economics teaching possibilities are within that life experience?

As high school students anticipate the senior prom, a senior trip, graduation, and other events unique to the senior year of high school that get potentially expensive, what economic lessons apply? If those seniors are taught in the August or September at the start of their senior year to save, save more, keep saving for the events of next May, the prom will not be a financial burden, and a life lesson in money management will have been learned through experience.

Students are real people living real lives right now. The economy is a dynamic system of real people with real decisions, plans, mistakes, successes occurring continuously. The real lives of students and the real dynamic nature of the economy can connect in the extreme economics classroom. When one of the most frequently and effectively used classroom resources is the life experience of students, combined with the wholesome knowledge, interests, and talents of students, the classroom can become a learning community. In this community the teacher is in charge, the teacher is responsible for causing learning, the teacher manages and leads; however, the teacher applies the life experience of students in the learning process, which helps convince students that this learning is real, is important, and is useful right now. The teacher makes connections between economics and the wholesome knowledge, interests, and talents of students to create motivation to learn by building on proper motivations the students already have. The result, similar to a successful business partnership, is a classroom community partnership in which students and the teacher create new learning together.

In the next chapter, we will explore more details, more minute-to-minute opportunities that alert teachers are given daily by students who eagerly and genuinely present teaching resources. The students may see what they are presenting as, for example, common conversations about their day-to-day lives, but extreme teachers see these presentations as powerful classroom resources.

5

STUDENT CONVERSATIONS, HOBBIES, AND DAILY LIVES: MORE RESOURCES FOR ANY TEACHER WHO LISTENS AND NOTICES

Sometimes the topic of economics unintentionally creates barriers for people who seek to understand economics. In the pursuit of detailed, comprehensive sophistication, perhaps, some explanation of economic ideas can get stuck in a maze of charts, graphs, equations, and awkward vocabulary. If a young student translates supply and demand as "A store has lots of ice cream, but nobody is buying it, so they have a buy-one-get-one-free sale and all of the ice cream is sold," then the student is showing some accurate and admirable understanding of supply and demand. The student can and will learn more, but if the goal is to learn, know, understand, think, and apply, this student is progressing toward the goal. In college, in graduate school, or in a high school advanced placement economics class, a complex depth and breadth of economic history, theory, analysis, and philosophy will be studied and learned. For much work with students in elementary, middle, and high school economics classes, the standard curriculum and the extreme economics approach will emphasize connections; real-life applications; experiences of students; and the wholesome knowledge, interests, and talents of students.

The ice cream explanation of supply and demand can certainly be used by an extreme economics teacher to Socratically lead that student and others to build on the ice cream idea; however, declare a small victory when the ice cream answer or a similar real-life answer is given. Economists would explain supply and demand in their complex and thorough language, as well they should. Ice cream is less complex, but it certainly relates to economics in general and supply and demand in particular.

Extreme economics is, of course, accurate in the study of money, business, career, investing, saving, vocabulary, and applications. Extreme economics is academically valid and challenging. Extreme economics is real, and that is one of the most important advantages of this approach to learning. A student whose real-life experience with a lemonade stand business, grass-cutting business, or fast-food restaurant part-time job is a resource used to make connections with the economics curriculum is a student who commits to learning in that class. The graduate school theory of widgets—those all-purpose imaginary products—has its place, but in K–12, let's be as real as possible to create as many right-now, right-here, today, real-life connections to inspire and cause learning.

In this chapter, we will listen to several conversations involving elementary school students, middle school students, and high school students. While reading these conversations, please think of ways that an extreme economics teacher could apply the topics of these conversations to the classroom study of economics. Think also of how the topics of these conversations could be the basis of connections between the life experiences of students and the money management truths that the survey research confirmed that children and teenagers need to learn. Similarly, notice how the wholesome knowledge, interests, and talents of students could be applied to build connections with a school's economics curriculum, including fundamental terminology or vocabulary.

Kristen and Katelyn are best friends. Their families live on the same street, so the girls have grown up together during all of their 10 years. They have played T-ball and soccer together at the nearby neighborhood park. They attend the same church, which is a short walk from their homes. They attended preschool together, and they have been in most classes with each other during kindergarten, first, second, and third grade. They are not in as many classes together this year, in fourth grade, but they still see each other often at school and in their neighborhood. They have not been allowed by their parents to get cell phones yet, but they do keep in touch with adult-supervised e-mail and instant messages. They both know a lot about computers.

"Hi, Kristen, wait a minute and I'll walk home with you. We can catch up with my brother at the middle school. My parents always tell me to walk home with Andy." Katelyn was pretty eager to leave.

"Yeah, I know. My parents always tell me to walk home with someone. They say things are just not as safe as when they were young. Hey, let's stop at the store and get something to drink. I'm so thirsty, and the only stuff to buy at school is fruit juice." Katelyn was annoyed by what Kristen said.

"That is so unfair, Kristen. We used to have soft drinks and stuff, but it changed. Our teacher told us that the grown-ups decided that children were getting unhealthy. Well, if some kids are fat and lazy, that's their problem. You and I play soccer and walk home and swim in the summer. We're healthy."

"Yeah, Katelyn. A few kids get fat and everyone suffers. Well, it's no big deal. We can get what we want at the store. They still sell the good stuff. Hey, there's your brother. Who is that boy with him?"

"Think he's cute? He's a new seventh grader. Look, we are just fourth graders, so don't dream too much. Andy and Taylor will walk with us because my parents say Andy has to walk with me. Come on, Kristen, let's catch up."

"Hey, Kristen. Hi, Katelyn. This is my friend Taylor. He's new at our school. He's a great soccer player." Andy seemed to be in a hurry, as he spoke quickly. "Listen, Katelyn, I know we have to walk home with you guys, but let's hustle. Taylor and I need to get back to school to help set up for the middle school carnival. It's tomorrow night and there is a lot of work to do."

That was fine with Katelyn. "Okay, but we need to make a quick stop at the store."

Taylor liked that idea. "Yeah, I'm hungry. Let's get to the store. I need some food so I can do all of that carnival work. Are you guys coming to the carnival?"

Kristen responded, "I hope so. I want to. My parents said that our whole family might go. My sister is in eighth grade at the middle school. I think she is staying after school today for volleyball practice. What's it cost to go to the carnival?"

Katelyn knew. "I read the middle school website. It said admission is $2, and that gets you in, plus a free t-shirt which some businesses donated. The activities are 50 cents each. There will be food and games and stuff. There is one pass that gives you unlimited games all night for $8. I think there is a family pass for $25 to let everyone in the family play games all night. Hey, Andy, when does the carnival open?"

"It's tomorrow night, 6 to 9. Hey, we're at the store. Let's make it fast."

Andy was more interested in getting home and back to school, but Taylor, Kristen, and Katelyn were looking at all of the snacks. In a few minutes, they had their after-school supplies paid for and were ready to begin the walk home.

Taylor had a question. "This new energy bar tastes just like a candy bar but costs a lot more. I bet it's no different than a candy bar. Andy, do you know anything about these?"

"Yeah. Actually, I do. Our health teacher told us all about those nutrition bars. She said there is nothing wrong with them but nothing great about most of them either. Our teacher would go crazy watching Kristen and Katelyn with those soft drinks. She says 'water, water, water.' Plus she tells us that soft drinks cost too much; she guesses that the $1 you pay for a soft drink costs about 10 cents for the drink and 10 cents for the bottle, so you give away 80 cents."

Katelyn and Kristen were not bothered. They finished their soft drinks, said they would call each other later, and each began their after-school routine of chores at home, homework, and playing at the park. Andy and Taylor gave each other 30 minutes to meet at the park and then go back to school. They both had math and computer homework to do, so they had to be home by 6, eat supper, and do the homework. Their families had already agreed to that schedule of the boys working at school from 4 to 6.

Katelyn and Kristen called each other about 4:30. Both had quickly finished their chores and homework. "Hey, Katelyn, let's play basketball at your house. I need to work on free throws."

"Neat idea. Come on over. See you in a few minutes." Katelyn talked to her mother for a few minutes and then went outside to wait for Kristen. Mom had asked about school and the middle school carnival. Now, it was time for free throw practice.

Kristen had an idea. "The carnival will have a free throw booth. We can win so many prizes if we practice. Let's try to hit five in a row."

Their practice was productive. Eventually, both girls hit five free throws in a row. Kristen wondered, "If we win all of those prizes, how does the school make money on the carnival?"

Katelyn had an idea. "Most people don't practice free throws, so most people do not win prizes. Plus, a lot of the prizes are donated by people or companies, so that's free. I heard they make a lot of money from the bake sale because people give them cakes and stuff. Whatever is sold is all profit. If they sell a lot of those family passes, that adds up. So, they make a lot of money. The work is done free, like Andy and Taylor working now."

Kristen dreamed. "I wish I could make money like the carnival does. Then I could pay for my own cell phone."

It was time for both girls to get back inside and clean up for supper at their homes. Thursday night at Kristen's was pizza night, and the pizza always arrived at 6:30. Katelyn and her family for years had children's choice on Thursday. Katelyn and Andy agreed that morning that their choice for tonight was chicken. Their father was bringing home a complete chicken meal from the nearby grocery store delicatessen. He said it was cheaper to buy it that way and have nothing to clean up than for everyone to take the time to shop, cook, and clean up.

At school on Friday, the elementary school students and the middle school students were excited about the carnival. Fridays at school often have lots of tests, and this was no exception, but one test really surprised Katelyn and Kristen. They have math class together, and today's math test had math problems to work, of course, but all of the problems were about the carnival. This test was actually enjoyable. That was new. The following questions were some of the math problems on the test.

1. It costs $1 to have your face painted at the carnival. If 1 face can be painted in 5 minutes, how many can be painted in an hour? At that rate, how much money could 1 person painting faces for 3 hours make for the carnival? How much would 3 people painting faces make in 3 hours?
2. If 120 family passes are sold at $25 each, how much money is taken by the total sales of the family passes?

3. In all, 210 people paid the admission price of $2 per person, instead of getting a pass for unlimited game play. How much money would be made from these ticket sales?
4. These 210 people also played some carnival games. The average amount spent on games was $5 per person. How much money total did these 210 people spend on games?
5. The concession stand that includes the bake sale will be busy. Let's predict that 630 people come to the carnival and that the average spent at the concession stand is $4 per person. How much money would be spent at the concession stand?
6. If the concession stand expenses are $500, how much profit would the concession stand make? Use your answer from Question 5.
7. Add the total money from three face painters, family passes, admission tickets, and games for individuals, plus concession-stand profit. Now, subtract $1,000 from that as the costs for the carnival. The costs are low because so many items were donated and all work was donated. How much money did the carnival make?

"Can you believe that math test? It was all about the carnival. I actually liked that test. That never happens." Kristen and Katelyn were eagerly talking at lunch.

"I know. It was so strange. I wish we did more math like that instead of what we always do. Hey, Kristen, what are you doing after school before the carnival?"

"Oh, I have to get an allergy shot, so my mother is picking me up. Then we have to get our dog. He's at the veterinarian for some shot and treatment. I think he has allergies, too. Dogs are so much fun, but they get expensive. So, Katelyn, see you at the carnival at 6."

"Yeah, I'll be there. I want to be first in line at the free throw game."

The middle school carnival certainly captured the attention of Kristen, Katelyn, Andy, and Taylor. One math teacher used the carnival for an academic advantage to intrigue students whose math skills were measured, applied, and developed through a test that used carnival calculations. Reflect now on additional ways that the real-life experience of a school carnival could be a teaching resource to help students master the economics curriculum and the money management skills from the research survey.

Now we are ready for the next conversation. Andy and Taylor have made much progress during middle school, and we join them soon after spring vacation of their eighth-grade year. Their thoughts are on the end of the school year, the start of summer, and then the start of high school.

Andy was really glad to see Taylor when the eighth graders got to the cafeteria for lunch. "Taylor, did you hear what those guys are doing on our graduation night? You know how high school students get limousines on prom night. Some eighth graders are doing that. They are getting a limousine. I think eight of them are going in on this."

Taylor was interested but surprised. "That's so cool. But doesn't it cost a lot of money? I mean, a lot?"

Andy was ready for that question. "Yeah. It's $160 an hour. Can you believe that? They reserved it for 3 hours, so that's almost $500. It won't be easy to pay for it."

Taylor had a guess. "Oh, it's probably the rich kids, and their families will pay for all of it. They never have to worry about money. They have all the money they need."

Andy interrupted. "That's just it. I talked to Tasha about it. She's one of the group getting the limousine. They have to pay for it themselves. Their parents will not pay any of it. That was the rule they set up. Eight students. They each have to come up with something like $60, just for the limousine. If they go to supper, they have to pay for that, too. I love it. The rich kids have to earn their own money."

Taylor continued his guess but with a new direction. "Maybe their parents finally decided to quit giving everything free to their children. Making them work for the money will show them how everyone else has to live. Hey, what's going on after school today? Isn't there some meeting you said something about?"

"Yeah. I'm going to that meeting. It's about getting a job this summer. Our school has people coming to talk to us about getting trained to be a lifeguard. For anybody who is 15 years old, it's a great job. I'll be 15 in a week. Aren't you 15 soon, Taylor?" Andy was hoping that Taylor would come to the meeting, too.

Taylor sounded interested. "Yeah. I'll be 15 next month. I'm not so sure that I want to be a lifeguard, but I'll go to the meeting. I think I heard on the announcements this morning that they would serve snacks at the meeting. So, yeah, I'll go, but I'm still not excited about being a lifeguard."

Andy was eager to convince Taylor. "Taylor, get real. Who goes to the swimming pool in the summer? If you are a lifeguard, you work at a swimming pool, you make money, and you get to see the girls who come to the pool. Can you think of a better job?"

Taylor was not convinced. "The job is not that easy. It's work. It's hot in the summer. The pool has to be cleaned. The children have to be told not to run. Let's go to the meeting, eat the snacks, and see what they tell us."

Andy got in the last word before they changed the subject. "Okay. I'll see you at the meeting. I'm going to be a lifeguard this summer. If you don't do this, you'll be sorry. You'll come to the pool and wish you could be a lifeguard. You can't wait until July to do this. It's April. It's time to plan for the summer. Take the training in May and make the money all summer. Hey, did you ever get your computer back in your room at home? It's been weeks since your mom took it away from you."

Taylor was ready. "Yeah, I got it back, sort of. I can use it, but it's in the family room right next to the kitchen and I can use it only a half hour every day. Plus, my mom or dad have to be in the room when I'm on the computer. It's better than nothing. Hey, yearbooks are going to be in soon. Did you buy one?"

Andy sounded annoyed. "No. They cost $25 and I wanted to order one, but I did not have the money. Nobody in my family would give me the money. I think I figured out a plan to get one. I talked to Mr. Franklin and Ms. Simpson—they sponsor the yearbook—I'm going to help them distribute the yearbooks and do other stuff when the yearbooks arrive. They said I could get a free book if I did 3 hours worth of work. Not bad. Did you buy one, Taylor?"

"Not exactly. I might buy one if they have any left over. Sometimes they order extra and don't sell all of them. Maybe I can buy one for half price on the last day of school. I think they did that last year to sell whatever was left over. I heard that the high school does not have a yearbook. They put it on DVD. Pictures, music, videos, and interviews. High school will be so much better than middle school. Not just the yearbook part. Everything is better in high school, like lunch. Here we are sitting in this tiny cafeteria with the same food every day. The high school has three or four different lines and all kinds of different food." Taylor spoke with the eagerness of many eighth graders who cannot wait for high school. Andy agreed.

"You are right, but those lunches will cost extra in high school. Pizza every day in the pizza line sounds good, but it will cost. So, you better get that lifeguard job this summer so you can save money for those fancy high school lunches."

Taylor laughed. "Yeah. Maybe you are right. Hey, it's time to go. Our teacher just got here. Can you believe how fast lunch goes? Well, see you at that meeting after school."

"Okay, Taylor. See you there. Your lifeguard career begins today."

Taylor and Andy are eighth graders. They would not be evaluated as experts in economics, but despite having no degree in economics and no formal corporate job title of senior vice president for economic analysis, Taylor and Andy are involved in economics, are affected by economics, are interested in economics, and, when taught economics using the extreme approach, can become experts in economics.

Extreme economics thrives on connections. Teachers lead students through classroom instructional experiences that connect the life experience of students with the economics curriculum. Extreme economics students are taught by extreme economics teachers who connect the wholesome knowledge, interests, and talents of students with the economics curriculum.

What topics from the conversation between Taylor and Andy could be used by an extreme economics teacher who kept informed of students' wholesome knowledge, interests, and talents? I will start a list and you can add to it, please.

1. Renting a limousine
2. Getting a summer job
3. Buying a yearbook
4.
5.
6.
7.
8.
9.
10.

Teachers usually do not eat lunch with Taylor, Andy, or other middle school students, so how will teachers hear the conversations that reveal the wholesome knowledge, interests, and talents of the students? Students begin talking to each other as soon as two students enter the school building. Students talk to teach other as they walk through the halls and into classrooms. Listen to those conversations. When it is proper, enter some of those conversations.

Take interest surveys. Go to extracurricular events. Visit churches that your students attend. Go to athletic events that your students participate in. Ask teachers who taught your students last year to share their insights about the students. When language arts teachers assign students a paper that is about hobbies, ask to read those papers.

Most students are generally willing, if not eager, to talk about themselves. Start those conversations. Ask those questions. Listen, really listen, to the answers and stories. Then apply what the student told you. The student who told you on Friday that she would travel to a soccer tournament over the weekend can give you a sports report on Monday. Also on Monday, you could do an economics activity about the cost of driving the 75 miles to the soccer tournament, driving the 75 miles back home, and all of the expenses associated with the trip and with the tournament. The student will be impressed with the application of economics to the soccer tournament. The other students can provide information about a wholesome activity of theirs over the weekend and can find connections with those activities and economics if their teacher leads them through purposeful instructional thinking, discussion, and activity.

The teacher is still in charge. The extreme economics teacher does not make the classroom an extension of the weekend or a continuation of the lunch cafeteria. The extreme economics teacher does use the life experiences of the students and the wholesome knowledge, interests, and talents of the students as one set of resources to cause learning. This learning is caused through instructional activities that make real connections between the real lives of students and the economics curriculum the students are to master.

What life experiences of high school students can apply to the study of economics? What wholesome knowledge, interests, and talents of high school students can be used in the extreme economics classroom? Cars, part-time jobs, sports, family, dating, college, career possibilities, cell phones, friends, favorite classes, school clubs, community activities, church, volunteer work, and any others that you can add to the list.

1.
2.
3.
4.
5.
6.
7.
8.
9.
10.

Andrea, Christie, and Melissa have been friends since elementary school. Their friendship has grown through the middle school years and high school years. These young ladies are juniors in high school and they ride to school together. Andrea's brother, Chad, is a senior in high school and he drives them to school each day. Their conversation on the way to school one morning in October will give many possibilities for extreme economics connections.

ANDREA: Did you guys study much for that U.S. history test? Mr. Johnson said it would be a lot like the advanced placement test we take next May. This is just too much work. Soccer practice every day. Soccer games. Homework. It's just October and I'll never get caught up.

CHRISTIE: I know, I can't keep up either. Well, actually I'm doing better now because I quit my job at the movie theater. Eighteen hours a week for minimum wage was such a waste. Our neighbors need me to baby-sit every Saturday, so I do that now. It's easy. I'm there from 8 in the morning until 3 in the afternoon. I make as much from that almost as from the movie place.

MELISSA: What do you do with the children for all that time?

CHRISTIE: They sleep until 11 or so. I do homework until they get up. Their parents own some store that is really busy on Saturday. At noon we go to that store and then usually go see a movie. Then it's 3 and their mother comes home. Easy work and good pay. They give me $8 an hour, pay for my lunch, and pay for us to go to a movie. They usually give me a tip so I end up with $60 for 7 hours of work, if you call it work.

MELISSA: If you ever need me to take your place, just tell me. If you can't go some Saturday, I'll go it. I've got to make money for car insurance and gas. I like driving, but it costs more than I realized.

CHAD: I know how you can make money. Baby-sit with old people. I know it sounds unusual, but some old people need somebody to help them at their home to clean the place or just keep them company. I know a college student who does that for $10 an hour.

ANDREA: The best way to make money is to make good grades in high school. If I can get that full scholarship to college, I save about $60,000. So all I do is study.

CHAD: That might work for you, Andrea. The rest of us need cash. I have to pay for that homecoming dance next week. Claire and I are going. She wants to go out for supper before the football game and then we'll go to the dance. That will cost me $50 or more.

CHRISTIE: If you help set up the gym for the dance, you can get free tickets. Friday after school for 2 hours is all you have to do. That saves you some money.

MELISSA: Is anyone going to that college fair next week? I heard that something like 60 colleges will have people there. I guess we have to start getting serious about college. Where are you going next year, Chad?

CHAD: I'll stay right here in town. With the big state university here, why go anywhere else? They have what I need and the price is not bad for in-state students.

CHRISTIE: What are you going to study in college?

CHAD: Probably, communications. I want to work in television or radio. Then all of you can watch my program or listen to me broadcast baseball games.

ANDREA: I've been listening to you forever, Chad. Is it okay if I watch a different program? Speaking of program, don't we have some guest speaker at school today?

MELISSA: That's right. We never have big assemblies, but the juniors get to hear some program today about college. There's a choice, I think. You can hear a speaker about college or the military or about vocational schools or about working full-time after high school graduation.

CHRISTIE: Chad, thanks for the ride to school. I have to hurry up and get to first period class early. I told Ms. Aguilar that I would help some ninth graders with their Spanish. It's my school service project. See you after school.

The four high school students enter their school of 1,900 students in 9th through 12th grade. They talk to friends, they get their books, they go to classes, they turn in homework, they experience a variety of teaching methods during the day, they relax for a few minutes at lunch, the juniors attend the assembly topic of their choice, they write down homework assignments, they take tests, they finish the day and go to soccer practice or to other activities or home. They have a rather typical day. What could make the day unusually productive and highly personal despite the common routines and the ordinarily impersonal procedures needed to manage the activities of 1,900 students and over 100 faculty, staff, administrators?

Despite the large size of many schools, interactions can be personal. Andrea, Christie, Melissa, and Chad are real people living real lives right now. If their teachers connect the life experiences of Andrea, Christie, Melissa, and Chad with the school's curriculum, the learning experiences can become more personal, real, meaningful, and worthwhile.

Imagine that the high school assembly about careers is followed by a survey in each class. The teacher and the students discuss career interests of the students. This takes the assembly topic from the general to the specific, from the large audience to the individuals. Perhaps a teacher could organize a discussion with a format similar to the one that follows:

These are the careers/jobs you said you are interested in:

Lawyer	Actor	Writer
Doctor	Radiology	Car design/engineering
Anesthesiologist	Orthodontist	Dentist
Surgeon	Mathematician	Inventor
Foreign missionary	Professional football/soccer player	
Technology	Robotics	Veterinarian
Preacher	Entrepreneur	U.S. military officer
Psychiatrist	Teacher	Marine biologist
Neurosurgeon	Model	Horse trainer
Psychologist	Aeronautical engineering	Equine veterinarian

Now, the question becomes, what will it take for you to reach that goal? Well, what have people who are in those careers successfully done to reach their goal?

1.
2.
3.
4.
5.
6.

Most employers will tell you that people skills are essential and that they are increasingly what makes the difference between getting a job and not getting the job or between success on the job and failure. What do you think they mean by *people skills*? How can you develop good people skills?

The process can become more personal and more precise. With eighth-grade economics students, I work with each student to set up their personal 9-year plan. This takes them through eighth grade, the 4 years of high school, and the 4 years after high school, which could be for college, military, technical/vocational school, and their first-full time jobs. The personal nature of this activity captivates each student. No two 9-year plans are identical. The students begin to envision a real path from where they are today to where they would like to be in 9 years.

During this process, the students do some computer research to explore websites of local high schools, a local college, and a local university. They are amazed at the possibilities, the challenges, the opportunities, the costs, the amount of work, and the increasingly demanding standards. I convince them that these opportunities can be prepared for, qualified for, and earned but that the process must begin now if it has

Table 5.1. Transylvania University and Ideas About Your 9-Year Plan

Year	*Achievements and Responsibilities*
2005–2006: 8th grade	
2006–2007: 9th grade	
2007–2008: 10th grade	
2008–2009: 11th grade	
2009–2010: 12th grade	
2010–2011	
2011–2012	
2012–2013	
2013–2014	

not begun already. Material that we use to begin the 9-year plan, thinking, and research is in Table 5.1.

1. What does the name Transylvania mean?
2. When was Transylvania founded? What does *founded* mean?
3. What's the list of Alumni Who's Who tell you about Transylvania?
4. What is the student-to-faculty ratio at Transylvania? What difference could this make?
5. "More than 96% of the tenured faculty hold the Ph.D. or highest degree in their field." What does that mean?
6. What does the word *major* mean for a college student?
7. What does the word *minor* mean for a college student?
8. From the list on the Academic Program page, what three majors would be of most interest to you and why?

Major reason it is of interest:

   a.

   b.

   c.

9. What is the answer to "What if I don't know what I want to major in?"
10. What is an internship? What is good about internships?
11. Activities and sports: Which would be of most interest to you?
12. 14-week Fall term, 14-week Spring term, 4-week May term—where have some of the May term classes been held recently?
13. What is graduate school?
14. What are some graduate schools listed that Transylvania graduates have attended?
15. What is the William T. Young Scholarship?
16. How much does it cost for a year at Transylvania?
    a. Tuition:
    b. Room and board:
    c. Total:
    d. Okay, that is a lot of money . . . how do you pay for it?
       (Transylvania University in Lexington, Kentucky, is the oldest college/university west of the Allegheny Mountains. The aforementioned questions are based on a brochure for prospective students. Much of this information and more information about this outstanding liberal arts school is at www.transy.edu.)

Economics—Computer Lab—Career Research

1. The job that you are most interested in:
2. Description of the job:
3. Responsibilities of people who have this job:
4. Qualifications and requirements for people who get this job:
5. Expected salary range:
   Note: Some people make less, some people make more.
   Note also: Money is only one way to measure "income" from a job.
6. Similar jobs:
7. Work duties, responsibilities, experience available now that could help lead you to the job you are more interested in:
8. Write the website addresses for job/career information that were provided:

   August 10, 2016

   Dear Dr. Babbage,

   Remember all of the work we did in economics class about our 9-year plan to get us to the job of our dreams or to the graduate school of our dreams. Well, I have good news to report. Here's what I have accomplished and here's how it was done.

Please do not just copy those activities and use them with your students. I did not copy those activities from another source and distribute them to students. I created those materials for my students to teach them economics based on what they need to learn and what I know about their life experiences and their wholesome knowledge, interests, and talents.

The students are fascinated with the 9-year plan for many reasons, including that it is personalized so each 9-year plan is unique. For some students it is their first serious look at the high school years and what can be accomplished then. It is also for some students the first realizations that what they are doing now or not doing now, what they are achieving now or not achieving now, is directly connected to what they will have the opportunity to do later or what they will not earn the opportunity to do later.

Students know when they are being taught in a personal way that is based on genuine concern for the student and when they are being processed through impersonal, generic, superficial routines. Some students have endured so many years of educational processing and school routines that they settled into the comfortable, easy, generic procedures of textbook chapters to read and worksheet blanks to fill in. Those procedures do not challenge students to think, motivate students to excel, and individually build upon the academic strengths of a student or resolve the academic weaknesses of a student. Those procedures fill the hours and the days at school, fill the grade book with numbers, fill report cards with ordinary grades, and the procedure is repeated next year with no break in the inertia.

Students prefer to be challenged and fascinated. Students will eagerly work when the work is worthwhile, meaningful, real, important, and connected to the life experiences of the student while also connecting to the wholesome knowledge, talents, and interests of students.

When school is reduced to a formula, a script, a process, then the result is processed education. When school is expanded to connect the infinite ideas, personalities, life experiences of students with the infinite knowledge of mankind in a curricular way, school can be very real, very lively, very productive, very extreme.

Here's another example of making school real and of making the study of economics extreme. Andrea, Christie, Melissa, and Chad will soon be on mailing lists of companies that would like to provide them with credit cards. A teacher could bring in a letter like that which the teacher received and read it to the students. How could the desired learning be caused in a more personal, more connected, more extreme way?

Through the efficiency of computers and word processing, an extreme economics teacher could create a letter that is personalized for each student. The letter will appear to be authentic. The letter will be addressed to Andrea, with another letter addressed to Christie, and with other letters—same content, different name—addressed to other students. Consider the following example and imagine what the impact could be if students studying credit were given a letter similar to this. The word *similar* is emphasized because teachers need to connect with the needs, strengths, and personalities of your students—as individuals and as a group.

April 1, 2007

Dear Andrea,

Congratulations! We are delighted to offer you the nation's finest credit card, the I Love My College Credit Card supreme. With each use of your new I Love My College Credit Card supreme, we will make a donation to your college or university library fund or athletics fund, your choice.

The new card is very convenient to use and is accepted almost everywhere. Your shopping will be made easier, and your payment schedule will be only once per month. If you pay your bill in full and on time, there will never be any interest charge. If your bill is not paid in full, the interest rate will be 1.5% per month, or 18% on an annual basis.

To sign up for your new card, just return the enclosed postcard or call us at 1-555-newcard. You could e-mail us at www.newcard now.iou. Even if you have other credit cards, this is the card that enables you to show your support for your favorite college! Plus, there is no membership fee and no annual fee for your first year of using the new card if you reply within one month. If you call by April 30 or e-mail by April 30, you will receive a free college calendar!!

We hope to hear from you soon. Thanks for giving us the opportunity to tell you about our new I Love My College Credit Card supreme. Go shopping soon with your new card!

Sincerely,
Deborah Jenkins, Vice President
Consumer Marketing

That introductory letter could be followed with a quick reality check about credit cards. The next day in class, Andrea is given a different letter. What important aspects of economics in general and credit in particular could be learned as Andrea reads, thinks about, and responds to this letter?

Dear Andrea,

Thank you for using your I Love My College Credit Card during the past month. We appreciate your business and your trust. Your unpaid balance at the start of your current billing cycle—February 22, 2008, through March 21, 2008—was $450.00, and during this billing cycle you charged $550.00, as detailed below. Your current total amount due is $1,006.75, which reflects the $450.00, $6.75 in interest on the $450, and the additional $550.00. Interest was 18% on an annual basis, for 1.5% for a month.

The minimum payment due by May 4, 2008, is $95.00. Interest will be charged on any unpaid balance as stated in the terms for your card.

Date	Item	Amount
3/2/08	Restaurant: Joe's Ribs	$45.00
3/10/08	Movie: Cinematix	$40.00
3/10/08	Store: Fashion Flair	$125.00
3/17/08	Car repair: Thomas Tires	$340.00
Total:		$550.00

1. What happens if you pay the full $1,006.75 by May 4, 2008?
2. What happens if you pay only $95.00 by May 4, 2008?
3. What mismanagement mistakes can people make with credit cards?
   a.
   b.
   c.
   d.
4. What wise management actions can people take with a credit card?
   a.
   b.
   c.
   d.

We know that Andrea, Christie, Melissa, and Chad are talented at talking. Teenagers can spend hours in conversation in person, on the telephone, especially cell phones, or via computer. A lesson about credit that includes a conversation could capture the attention, the thinking, and the reaction of students in ways that generic, superficial school processes cannot. Here's an example, and while reading please think of ways that conversation case studies similar to this could be used to cause learning in an extreme economics classroom.

SHAWN: "Yeah, well, I have three credit cards. I use one to the limit and then I use another one to that limit. I still have another card, and if I get to the limit on it, I'll just call them and ask if they can increase the limit." Shawn talked about this with no real concern at all.

TASHA: "You can't be serious. You are asking for lots of problems. You still owe the money. Don't you pay anything on these credit card bills when they arrive? Don't you have to make a minimum payment or something?" Tasha seemed worried about how her brother was managing his money.

SHAWN: "It's no big deal. I'm not worried about it. It will work out. Why are you so worried about this?"

TASHA: "Well, credit cards just make you think you have money when you don't have it. Writing a check is more honest if you do the math right. A debit card takes the money out of your account instantly and transfers it electronically to the store's account. Still, cash is the only way to really know if you can afford something." Tasha was serious.

SHAWN: "Come on. Who wants to carry a bunch of cash? It can get lost or something else. Credit cards make it easy."

TASHA: "Yeah, credit cards make it easy to spend too much money, to get stuck with lots and lots of interest charges, and to get in debt something awful. Just take your credit cards and cut them up, pay them off, and quit using credit."

List three problems with credit cards:

1.
2.
3.

For people who do use credit cards wisely and who avoid any credit card problems, what credit card rules do they follow? List three:

1.
2.
3.

Explain why you agree with Shawn or Tasha. In your answer, include three reasons why you agree with one person and include one reason why you disagree with the other person.

Agree:

1.
2.
3.

Disagree:

1.

Throughout a school day, weekend day, or vacation day, students encounter economics, interact with economics, and are affected by economics. The extreme economics teacher will apply these life experiences of students to cause learning of the economics curriculum. Let's think of a high school ninth grader, Kim, on a school day and from the moment the alarm clock goes off to the moment Kim goes to sleep, about 16 hours later—what interactions does Kim have with economics?

1. The alarm clock was purchased recently at a local store. The clock was on sale.
2. Kim's alarm clock wakes her up, not with a clanging or buzzing alarm noise, but with the sounds of her favorite radio station.
3. Kim has to get out of bed to reach the alarm clock. In the time since the clock went off and the time Kim turns the alarm clock off, she hears two commercials. One is for a concert she really hopes to attend and the other is for a new 16-screen movie complex she would like to go to soon.
4. Kim enters the bathroom and, without noticing it, is facing about 15 products that have effective marketing programs. Kim is loyal

to her brands but never gives it much thought. Toothpaste, mouthwash, contact lens solution, hairspray, soap, shampoo, hair conditioner, skin lotion, cosmetics, perfume, deodorant, facial tissue, and many others are product categories for which Kim has a clear preference.

5. Kim is not moving too quickly, but she does manage to finish a shower and get dressed. Her clothes are not expensive but are known brands, except for shoes. Her family goes to a shoe outlet because the products are high quality with a slight imperfection in appearance that nobody can see. The store always has 50% or higher discounts.
6. Breakfast is a bowl of cereal, milk, and a granola bar. The cereal is a store's brand because Kim's mother thinks the name brands of cereal cost too much.
7. Kim notices the commercial on the morning news on television. It's about that new movie place. The pictures look great. Kim really wants to go there this weekend, but her father always says that going to see a movie when it opens is wasting money. He says to wait two months and then see the movie at the discount theater. Kim thinks that the thrill is not just seeing the movie but being seen at the new movie place and being one of the first people to see any new movie. Kim wonders if Dad remembers what it was like when he was 14. Did movies exist then?
8. Kim rides to school with her brother, Billy, who is a senior in high school. Billy recently bought a used car that he is very proud of. His fast-food part-time job, including what he saved working extra jobs the past two summers, pays for the car payment, insurance, and gasoline. The car takes every dollar he makes.
9. At school Kim sees signs for the video yearbook and the printed yearbook. Each costs $25 or both for $40. That sounds like a lot of money to Kim. She decides to read Billy's yearbook instead of getting her own.
10. Two friends ask Kim if they can borrow money from her for lunch. These two friends never pay back a loan. Kim smiles and says no. The friends ask again. Kim says no again. The conversation ends.

Now, please expand the list. Think of what Kim will do, experience, encounter during the rest of the day at school, on her way home, and at home. Then think of how those regular daily occurrences could directly, creatively, and effectively connect with economics.

11.
12.
13.
14.
15.
16.
17.
18.
19.
20.

Let's make Kim the star of a case study. The following case study could be personalized for each student, and the circumstances could be easily modified to match the life experiences and wholesome knowledge, interests, and talents of your students.

KIM: HARD WORK AND HARD LESSONS

Money. Economics is all about money. Life is about much more than money, but if you get the money part of life right, the rest of life goes better.

I'm 14 years old. What can I do to make money? In 4 years from now I will graduate from high school and then go to college. How does anyone pay for college? One textbook for one college class can cost $100 now. When I go to college, that book will cost even more. So, I might have to spend over $1,000 per year in college just for the books I will need. The tuition at public universities in my state is going up about 14% next year. If that keeps up during the next 4 years, college would cost me almost twice as much as it costs now. I can just hear it. "Hi, Kim, we would like for you to attend our university, the best public university in the state, as a member of the class of 2014. The tuition for your freshman year will be $14,000. Yes, it used to be a lot less than that, but costs went up. We are still much less than some private colleges with tuition costs of $30,000 to $50,000 per year."

In 2 years, when I am 16 years old, I want to learn how to drive a car. I'll get my driving permit and then I'll get my driving license. Cars cost a lot of money. I saw a sign in the back window of a car yesterday. It said "For Sale, $1,200." Where would I get that much money to buy a very, very used car? Then where do I get the money for gasoline? Three dollars per gallon now. By the time I drive, it will be $4 per gallon or more.

College is going to cost more. Cars will cost a lot. Gasoline will keep costing more and more. What am I supposed to do? Just when I am ready to start doing all of this, it all starts to cost more than ever.

What do you mean, "Get a job"? I'm 14 years old. What job can I get? Baby-sit? Maybe. Cut grass? Well, yeah, I can do that during the summer. Rake yards when the leaves fall off trees and then shovel snow in winter? Yeah, I can do that in the fall and in the winter. I could make some money doing all of that, but I need to make even more. Is there any other way I could make money? I want to do this the right way; I just want to do it now and in a big, big way.

Entrepre-what? Entrepreneur? You are telling me to become something I can barley pronounce and that I have never heard of. What is an "entrepreneur"? Oh, that's what it is. You mean like the man who started Microsoft and is now the richest man in the country? I get it. He had a good idea, he made his idea into a product, and he has sold his product to millions of people.

Well, since I'm 14 years old, I probably am not going to compete with Microsoft yet. I need something closer to home that I can do and closer to my skills. What am I good at? This might sound surprising, but I'm a great cook. I just got interested in cooking because my grandmother was the best cook in the world. I used to spend part of every summer with our grandmother. She lived on a farm in Tennessee. We would watch my grandmother—we called her Nana—make these amazing meals. She explained how she made everything from homemade bread to desserts. I can cook. I sometimes fix the meals for our family for holidays or for family gatherings. Still, what can a 14-year-old do with cooking skills to make money?

Open a what? A lemonade stand? That is not very fancy cooking. Well, yeah, maybe I could sell more than lemonade. I bake great brownies, perfect chocolate chip cookies, and, the truth is, I'm an expert with cakes. My grandmother used to make old-fashioned lemonade. I guess

I could do that. It was a lot of work, but it was better than anything from a packaged mix of lemonade powder.

Well, this is worth some serious thought. What would I have to do before I could open my lemonade stand business? Sure, I can think about that and make a long list of everything that would have to be done before I could open the lemonade stand business. Here's my list:

1.
2.
3.
4.
5.
6.
7.
8.
9.
10.

It is early June and school has been out for 2 weeks. It is a hot day and everything is ready for me to open my lemonade stand. I decided that I needed a business partner, so my brother, Billy, is working with me, but he has another job, so he can help just a little. Funny, he stayed longer than he planned because some friends of his stopped by. Then his girlfriend stopped, and she said Billy was so sweet to help his sister. Billy promised to help again tomorrow.

Here's what happened at our lemonade stand on the first day we were open for business:

1.
2.
3.
4.
5.
6.
7.
8.
9.
10.

So, after the first day of business, we were really tired. We had been very, very successful with our business, but it was a super hot summer day and we are ready for some time off. I know, time off means that we don't make more money, so we made all the plans we needed to be ready to open our lemonade stand for the next day. Here's what we had to do to get ready for tomorrow:

1.
2.
3.
4.
5.
6.
7.
8.

This is hard work. Are we going to have to do this every day? Sure, we made a lot of money yesterday, but when do we get some time off from all of this work? Oh, so entrepreneurs don't get much time off? I may have to rethink this entrepreneur plan, but I'm going to do this for a week at least then see what Billy and I think.

Students are real people living real lives right now. Students interact with economics many times every day. Those interactions are real, so there is no need to use generic, ordinary, prefabricated instructional materials when students bring such vivid life experiences that can be a convincing catalyst toward mastery of economics.

In the next three chapters, we will experience a detailed journey as we visit a day in the life of an elementary school student, a middle school student, and a high school student.

6

A DAY IN THE ECONOMIC LIFE OF AN ELEMENTARY SCHOOL STUDENT

"But it's not easy being 9 years old. My older brother and my older sister tell me what to do. You and mom tell me what to do. My teachers tell me what to do. I really like my friends because we never tell each other what to do."

Zach's father listened closely and then had an idea. "Zach, I understand what you are saying. There are a lot of people who tell a 9-year-old what to do. Let's try this. I'll pick you up today after school and then take you to work with me for the rest of the day. I think you'll enjoy watching how we do our jobs."

Zach was thrilled. "Wow. That will be so neat. Can I stay and watch the news broadcast?"

"Sure. That's exactly what we'll do. Your school dismisses at 3:00 and we'll get to the television station about 3:30. That gives us time to get an after-school snack for you. The local news is broadcast from 5:00 through 6:30. The station is a very busy place right before the news and during the news. Now, you finish breakfast and get ready for school. I'm taking you to school today because you have that big history project you created. It's way too big to carry on a school bus. John always drives himself to high school and he's taking Jennifer to her middle school. Mom will be back this afternoon from that business trip to Atlanta. So, we're set for the day. See you in 10 minutes ready to go to school."

Zach's father smiled as his 9-year-old son jumped from the table where they had eaten breakfast. Mr. Brown's 18-year-old son, John, and 14-year-old daughter, Jennifer, finished breakfast a few minutes earlier and would soon leave for school after making sure that they looked just right. Mr. Brown wondered if middle school and high school had always been fashion shows.

"I'm ready, Dad. This fort I made for history class is pretty big, but it fits in the backseat. Thanks for taking me to school. I'd never get this project on the bus."

"Okay, Zach. John is driving Jennifer to school. They just left for school. I'll be ready to take you in 1 minute. Do you have lunch money?"

"It's in my account at school. This is Wednesday. I have $6 in my account. Lunch is $2 each day, so that will get me through the week." Zach wanted to show that he was managing his account well, because his father put $5 in Zach's bank savings account for each week that Zach correctly managed his lunch money. The school's lunch accounting system was on computer, and parents and guardians could access their children's accounts via the Internet, just as they could also check grades via the Internet.

"That sounds perfect, Zach. We're ready, let's go."

As Mr. Brown drove to school, he and Zach talked about their plan for after school. Zach was beginning to realize one of the reasons he was going to the television station where his father was the general manager. "You mean everyone tells everyone else what to do? The grown-ups boss each other around?"

"Good thinking, Zach. You'll see a lot of people giving instructions to the people they work with. It looks easy, but there is a lot that has to happen to get the news program on television. You've been to the station before but not to watch the actual production and broadcast of the news. Okay. We're at your school. Need any help with that fort?"

"No, thanks. I can get it. Hey, there's Matthew. I'll get him to carry my book bag so I can carry the fort. Thanks, Dad. See you after school."

"Bye, Zach. Have a great day."

Zach did have a great day at school. The history projects were taken to the library and put on display. The library looked like a museum, which was the intention. This is Third-Grade History Museum Day at Zach's elementary school. Several college professors of history were guests. They were observing the projects and were going to talk with the students.

Several computers in the library were displaying websites from museums from throughout the country. As students and teachers visited the library, they could see the projects and hear presentations about them as they talked to the third-grade students about their creations. Admission to the museum was free, but each student had to earn an admission ticket. Teachers had given all students history questions to answer in recent days, and after a student correctly answered five questions, he or she earned a museum admission ticket.

The librarian had sent a press release about the third-grade museum to local newspaper, radio, and television reporters. A newspaper photographer took many pictures of the projects. A television reporter from the station where Zach's father works came with a videographer to film a story. His father had not told Zach about this, so it was an exciting surprise for Zach. The reporter talked to the librarian, a teacher, and three students, plus had lots of film, including a close-up of Zach's fort.

During math, Zach and all of the students did history math. All of the math problems were about the periods and the places the projects dealt with. Some of the math problems were about prices paid for products people used in earlier times. Some math problems were about the real museums and how much it costs to go to a museum, plus how much people who work at a museum can make in their jobs.

All of the other classes had some connection with the third-grade history projects. Reading class included a history chapter. Science class was about scientific ideas from many years ago. Even gym class included dances people did in earlier times. The whole day was really interesting to Zach, but he was most amazed with lunch. The cafeteria staff arranged an old-fashioned home-style meal with traditional foods that the teachers had told them were common in the colonies during the early and mid-1700s. The vegetables, the breads, the desserts, and the meat were really good and made some students wonder if old-fashioned cooking was better than microwave food or fast food from the drive-thru. Zach wondered if a meal like they had at lunch was expensive. He paid his usual $2 for a lunch, but he thought he got a lot more than $2 worth of food.

The day passed quickly and soon Zach was in his last class of the day. His history teacher had one last surprise. She came into class dressed just like people dressed in the 1940s. Some students had done their history projects about World War II. So this teacher was taking everyone back to the 1940s. She played music and parts of radio programs from the 1940s. She had two newspapers from 1943 and 1948 that showed prices from grocery stores, and everyone was amazed at the prices versus current prices. The teacher explained that some products were not available or were limited during World War II.

When the school day ended, Zach was quickly out the front door of the school to join his father, who was interested in Zach's day.

"Dad, it was so cool. The library looked great. It was just like that museum you and mom took us to in Washington."

Dad was impressed. "You mean the Smithsonian? Your school library looked like the Smithsonian. I can't wait to come see it tomorrow night at your school's family night."

"You'll love it, Dad, but you actually get to see it today. A reporter from your television station came to our school to see the museum. Maybe that will be on your news program tonight."

"Let's hope so, Zach. Let's stop in this store to get a snack for you. Get something healthy, even if you get something else that is not so healthy."

Zach knew what to get. He really did prefer water to any soft drink. What else should he get? Chips, cookies, candy bar, granola bar? Then he saw a package of trail mix. He had that last summer at a scout camp and really liked it. So, water and trail mix. That should be healthy enough. Zach's father also got a bottle of water and paid for everything. On the way to the television station, Zach and his father talked about what they had seen in the store. Water was 99 cents per bottle, but the sale price of the brand of water they chose was two bottles for $1.50, so they saved money. The trail mix was $1.49 for a package, but it had an instant peel-off coupon with 50 cents on it, so that made the price 99 cents. They agreed that there were many ways to save money if people just thought about it.

"Thanks, Dad. I was really hungry. Thanks for getting me at school. What are we going to do first at the TV station?"

"Well, how about your homework. What do you need to do for school for tomorrow?"

"Just math. I have 15 math problems to do." Zach sounded confident.

"Okay. You can use my office to get your math finished. There are two people I'd like you to meet. Our sales director will explain to you how we make money from selling TV time for commercials. Then our personnel manger will talk to you about careers in television. After that you and I will go to the studio to watch the five o'clock news broadcast."

Zach was really excited. "Wow. I'll do the math in no time. Do you think we can talk to the reporter who came to my school?"

"Sure. While you do the math homework, I'll find that reporter. See you in about 15 minutes, son."

The discussions about advertising sales and television careers were interesting to Zach. What he liked best was talking to the reporter and seeing how the story about the school's museum project was being prepared for the news. The reporter had a question for Zach that he never expected. "Zach, here's an idea. Instead of me introducing the story, you could do it. The news anchor announcer can say, 'Our next story is about an elementary school library being transformed into a history museum.' Then, to introduce the story, 'We have with us Zach Brown, a student who was involved in the museum project.' Are you interested?"

"Sure! I'd love to do that. I get to be on TV. Thanks!" Zach hugged his father and then began working with the reporter to be sure everything was perfect. A trade of winks between Mr. Brown and the reporter confirmed that this plan would work.

Zach's debut on television news was flawless. He was comfortable in front of the camera. He thanked his teachers, and he praised the students for the work they did. Then he smiled at the reporter and said, "Back to you for more on this story," and the reporter completed the work. Is Zach on his way to a career in television? Time will tell, but he certainly is on his way to another great day at school tomorrow.

Zach is not the only student in his third-grade class or in his elementary school whose day included events and experiences, ideas and observations, questions and answers that can connect with economics. Zach's life experiences during this one day can be productive resources for any extreme economics teacher. The wholesome knowledge, interests, and talents applied in the history projects provide more resources for ex-

Table 6.1. Examples of Connections Between Zach's Day and the Financial Wisdom From the Research Survey for This Book

Research Findings	*Connections With Zach*
1. Save, save more, keep saving	Zach and his father found discounts when they got snacks after school.
2. Start saving now	Zach's lunch account at school is managed by Zach to keep $2 for each day. For each week he balances this account, his father puts an extra $5 in Zach's savings account.
3. Have a money plan	Zach manages his lunch account to keep $2 for each day. Zach learned about the television station's finances from the advertising sales manager.
4. Credit is deceptive	Zach's lunch account begins with a $10 deposit each Monday. If he runs out of money before Friday, the cafeteria manager knows not to extend credit—that rule is from Zach's father. So far, Zach has always had $2 for each day.
5. Live within your means	Managing the lunch account even on days when an extra slice of pizza for $1 is difficult. Zach knows the limit is $2 daily. He cannot spend $1 on extra pizza each day.
6. Life is not about money	The time with his father, the history museum project, and the television station adventure were the best parts of the day, and they did not cost money; but good money management helped the day go well.
7. The measurement of economics is math	Zach completed math problems. Zach and his father analyzed the after-school snack prices. Zach learned the cost to advertise on the TV station's programs. Zach learned the possible income with various TV station jobs and careers.
8. Get the best and the most education	Zach did excellent work on his history project.
9. Develop a strong work ethic	Zach was required to do his math work before he could tour the TV station.
10. People are more important than money	Zach's father taught this to Zach by his example of spending so much time with Zach. When he was on television, Zach sincerely thanked and acknowledged teachers and other students for their work on the history project museum.

treme economics instruction. Table 6.1 shows examples of connections between Zach's day and the financial wisdom from the research survey for this book.

Can an extreme economics teacher also connect Zach's life experiences and his wholesome knowledge, interests, and talents with the basic, fundamental vocabulary of economics? The terms my eighth graders must master are listed in Table 6.2, with connections to Zach, but as you think of additional connections, please include those ideas.

Zach's life experiences and his wholesome knowledge, interests, and talents connect directly with the research survey results, plus with the vocabulary of economics. Extreme economics uses these connections to make learning economics real. Zach and other elementary school students are already experiencing economics each day, so that experience becomes an unlimited classroom resource that makes learning for students much more personal, individualized, meaningful, fascinating, and real. The extreme economics approach is efficient and effective for teachers because it works. Students eagerly do work that is real, that connects to their lives, that connects to what they are already motivated by and dedicated to.

The following materials are thought starters for teachers. These materials have worked with my students, but I create new materials and new activities for each group of students because each student is unique and each class is unique. Please read through these materials so they can be catalysts for your creativity.

One more point about Zach's day. Not every town has a television station. Not every student has a parent or guardian working at a television station. Other work places could be just as interesting and just as connected with economics as is a television station. Identify the resources within your school, within your community, within the jobs of parents and guardians of your students, and use those resources to make extreme economics connections.

There are many ways to define *economics* and there are many topics that are part of the overall concept of and activity of economics; however, no matter what definition is used, no matter what economics concept is considered, and no matter what economics activity you participate in, there is one certainty: Economics is about money.

Table 6.2. Terms Eighth Graders Must Master

Economic Vocabulary	*Connections With Zach*
1. The law of supply and demand	The trail-mix instant coupon may have been needed to sell excess supply and to increase demand.
2. Production	How are television programs and commercials produced? How is trail mix produced?
3. Distribution	What steps are involved in getting the bottles of water from their source to the store shelf?
4. Consumption	Dad and Zach drank their water. Zach consumed his trail mix.
5. Productivity	Zach's teachers accomplished more teaching and learning more efficiently by connecting the history project to many subjects and classes.
6. Technology	The television station broadcasts the news.
7. Competition	At the store, Zach considered several products for his after-school snack.
8. Specialize	Zach learned of jobs at the station, where each person has precise duties in which he or she specializes.
9. Money	How much does it cost to broadcast a commercial on the local news program? Why was the price of water discounted with purchase of two bottles?
10. Scarcity	There was almost not enough time in the morning to get ready for school and to get breakfast.
11. Profit	How does the television station make money in addition to selling time for commercials to be broadcast?
12. Land, labor, capital	The history projects showed how earth, work, and money were applied in different ways, by various people in a variety of places and times.
13. Risk	The store where Zach got his after-school snack faces risks every day, as customers have options of other stores.
14. Opportunity cost	Zach did not spend an extra dollar from his lunch account for an extra slice of pizza today, because he would not have enough money for lunch later in the week.
15. Interdependent	The teachers worked together to make the history project a theme in many classes.
16. Advertisement	The television station sells commercial time and broadcasts advertisements.
17. Finances	How much money does Zach have for lunch each week, how much does lunch cost each day, and which bonus can Zach earn if he manages this account correctly during a week?

THE WAYS OF MONEY

Ways that people legally acquire money
Ways that people sensibly make use of money (Note: Spending is not the only option and is not the first option.)
Ways that people invest money
Ways that people save money
Ways that people manage money
Ways that people mismanage money
Ways that people plan for future needs
Ways that businesses use money to provide goods and service that will, they hope, convince you to shop there and spend money there
Ways that government acquires money and uses money
Plus, much more about money, jobs, business, charities, investments, bills, checks, credit cards, banks, and more

So, to begin, what is money?

What is the first rule about money?

P.S. Needs are much more important than wants. Saving is much more important than spending.

Money mistakes:

1.
2.
3.
4.
5.
6.
7.
8.

Money wisdom:

1.
2.
3.
4.
5.

6.
7.
8.
9.
10.

MONEY, IDEAS, QUESTIONS, AND CALCULATIONS

1. Define the word money:
2. What is the purpose of money?
3. What words would you associate with money?
   a.
   b.
   c.
   d.
4. Write two questions you have about money:
   a.
   b.
5. Is a check money? Reason/evidence:
6. Is a credit card money? Reason/evidence:
7. Is a gift card money? Reason/evidence:
8. Is a postage stamp money? Reason/evidence:
9.

Cost to skate	Number of people skating	Total admission
$5.00	200	a.
$4.00	250	b.
$3.00	350	c.
$2.50	500	d.
$2.00	500	e.

10.

Price of 2-liter	Number sold	Total sales	Cost to store	Profit each	Total profit
$1.50	20	$30.00	$1.00	.50	$10.00
$1.25	30	$37.50	$1.00	.25	$7.50
.99	50	$49.50	.79	.20	$10.00
.79	110	$86.90	.69		
.69	130	$89.70	.64		

11. The magical math of an IRA. Assume that this deposit will grow at 10% per year, doubling in value every 7.2 years.

Year	Value	Year	Value	Year	Value
2010	$2,000	2031.6		2053.2	
2017.2		2038.8		2060.4	
2024.4		2046.0			

Economics is all about money. One reality about money is that work equals pay. In this class, students have been paid extra points for several reasons, including doing great work on a test, doing great work on homework, and asking a brilliant question or giving a brilliant answer to a question. Economics is also about getting in the habit of Save. Save more. Keep saving. As we earn extra points for our Individual Reward Account, we save those points for two weeks and then we redeem them for rewards.

The reasons I think it is a good idea for us to get paid are

1.
2.
3.
4.

The reasons I think it is a good idea for us to build up points in an Individual Reward Account are

1.
2.
3.

Explain three similarities of getting paid in this class and earning IRA points with how the economy in our society really works.

1.
2.
3.

MONEY AND SPORTS

The economics of March Madness. Select one of the following options:

1. Design a new indoor sports arena.
    a. Draw the exterior of the building; include the name of the arena and tell why that is the name.

   b. Draw the interior of the building. What is the seating capacity? Why?
   c. List and describe the five most important improvements your arena has that make it better than other arenas.
   d. Select one event and tell what the prices would be for three different locations of seats; give a reason for each price.
   e. Design the homepage of the website for the new arena; include five link boxes.
   f. Write a 30-second commercial about the grand opening of the arena and the first sporting events that will be held there: the March Madness 2010 NCAA men's basketball final tournament, 1 week after a NCAA women's basketball regional tournament.
2. Design the ultimate sporting goods, sporting souvenirs, sports everything store.
   a. Draw the exterior of the store; include the name of the store and tell why that is the name.
   b. Draw the interior of the store—show each department, aisles, checkout counters, and other details.
   c. List and describe the five most important advantages your store has over other competitors.
   d. Design the newspaper ad that tells people about the grand opening of your store; include products, prices, directions to the store, and coupons, plus information about the grand opening event.
   e. Design the homepage of the website of your store; include five link boxes.
   f. Write the 30-second commercial telling people about your new store.
3. Create a new TV sports network.
   a. Tell the name of the new network and why that is the best name.
   b. Tell the name of six weekly or daily programs you will have on the network; describe each of the programs and what audiences you expect to attract with these programs.
   c. List four live sporting events that your network will broadcast and explain why you think each of these events will be watched by large audiences.
   d. List and explain the four advantages your network has over other sports and TV networks—tell why viewers will be impressed with each of these four advantages.

e. Design the homepage of the website for your new TV network; include five link boxes.
f. How will you advertise your new network so people know about it, ask their cable provider to have it, and then watch it: radio, television, or print? Pick one and create the ad/commercial you would use to introduce your network to potential viewers.

P.S. When we discuss these projects in class, we will relate them to the economics core content vocabulary terms. As you create your project, think of how it relates to our favorite terms:

Economics core content term	How it relates to my project
1. Law of supply and demand	
2. Production	
3. Distribution	
4. Consumption	
5. Productivity	
6. Technology	
7. Competition	
8. Specialize	
9. Money	
10. Scarcity	
11. Profit	
12. Land, labor, capital	
13. Risk	
14. Opportunity cost	
15. Interdependent	
16. Advertisement	
17. Finances	

MONEY AND TELEVISION

First, think of television shows that you enjoy. Second, think of television shows that are not your favorites but that you know that a lot of other people like. Third, overall, what types of television programs seem to be most popular?

1. Create a new television program. Before you give it a name, (a) think of the type of program it will be; (b) the characters who will be in the program (not the actors and actresses but the characters who are portrayed in the program); (c) who the target audience is, what that means, who the show is designed to attract as viewers; and (d) some possible plots for episodes of the show. Now, describe the program answering (a), (b), (c), and (d).
2. Now, give the program a name. Why is that a great name for the new television program?
3. Create the pilot episode, which is the first episode of the new program. Outline/describe/write about three scenes from the episode: What are the characters doing? What are the characters saying? What issues come up? What is amusing, if anything? What is complicated, if anything? What else happens?
4. What is it about this show that will attract people in the target audience to watch?
5. Think of three products that would pay to have their commercials shown on this program. Why would those products pay to advertise on this program?
6. Think of three reasons why one of those products in Question 5 would pay more to have one of the show's characters using or mentioning that product during a scene in the television program.
   a.
   b.
   c.
7. Write one 30-second commercial from one of the products you mentioned in Question 5. Write the audio portion word-for-word and describe the video.
8. Design the website for the new program.

MONEY AND FOOD

Invent a new cereal. Think of an idea for a new cereal that, in at least one way, is different from and better than current cereals. Think, also, of the people this cereal is intended to appeal to so that the new cereal is designed with that group in mind.

1. Give the cereal a name. What does the name communicate about this new cereal? Explain why this is the perfect name for the cereal.
2. Design the package for the new cereal. Design all sides of the package. Include (a) the name of the cereal, (b) graphics on the front and on the back, (c) nutritional information, (d) website address, and (e) 800 number. You will also include either (1) a recipe that uses the cereal or (2) a promotional offer that gives the consumer an item free or a reduced price with purchase of the cereal.
3. Describe the cereal: shape, color, taste, ingredients, and any special benefits the cereal provides.
4. Design the website for the cereal. Show what the initial screen would look like and list all of the topics/links that would be available.

Your choice—select one of the following:

1. Create an eight-page issue of a new magazine—included in the eight pages are the cover, the inside front cover, the back cover, and the inside back cover—that would be of interest to elementary school students. The magazine will include all of the following (and more if you add more):
   a. The front cover showing words and pictures about the contents and including the name of the magazine
   b. Advertisements on the inside front cover, the inside back cover, and the back cover
   c. Two or three articles total on pages 1–4
   d. Some ads on pages 1–4
2. Create an eight-page catalogue for (a) a sporting goods store or (b) a car dealership. The catalogue will include all of the following (and more if you add more):
   a. The front cover showing words and pictures about the contents, plus the name of the company sending the catalogue
   b. Pictures, prices, advice, ordering information, and special deals
   c. A letter from the president of the company to the reader of the catalogue—this goes on the inside front cover

Yes, you may cut and paste . . . you may draw . . . you may use pictures . . . you may interview people . . . you may include letters from readers. Be sure that everything you include makes sense, is spelled correctly, is rated G, and shows that you put some solid thinking into your work.

Zach's sister, Jennifer, is 14 years old, and she is very much a middle school eighth grader. In chapter 7, we will spend a day with Jennifer and see how her life experiences and her wholesome knowledge, talents, and interests can connect with extreme economics.

7

A DAY IN THE ECONOMIC LIFE OF A MIDDLE SCHOOL STUDENT

Friends. If you ask Jennifer Brown what she likes best about eighth grade, the answer is her friends. Seeing her friends, talking with her friends, being with her friends, making plans with her friends, and hearing the latest middle school social news from her friends are the best parts of school.

What about classes to attend, books to read, tests to take, homework to do, projects to finish, and all of the other work associated with school? "Yeah, all of that is important," Jennifer admits, "and I make good grades. My parents insist that I make the honor roll. School is not so hard, but all of the work does keep me from doing some things with my friends. The best part of school is friends. Tasha, Shawn, Brian, Julie, Robert, Whitney, Andrea, Christie, Vickie, Martha, Hunter, Taylor, and everybody else. They are the best. We talk all the time. We tell each other everything. I know I have to do all the school work stuff, but the neatest part of school is friends."

Soon after the alarm clock awakens Jennifer, she starts to think about her plans for the day. Her mother is out of town at a business conference in Atlanta, but she will be back this afternoon to pick up Jennifer at school at 2:00 to go to the orthodontist. Jennifer smiles as she realizes she will miss her seventh-period class today because of leaving school early. Science class is . . . well, it is just not Jennifer's favorite subject.

The experiments they do in class are interesting, but Jennifer is not going to be a scientist. She is going to be a writer, just like her mother. Ms. Brown writes books for children, actually, really young children. She writes books that families can use with children aged 4–8 to help them learn everything from colors to sharing, from counting to being polite. The business conference Ms. Brown is attending is about books for children.

Jennifer is going to write fiction books for middle school girls. Language arts class is her favorite class every year. She reads a lot. She writes a lot. She talks a lot. Jennifer is at her best when she is communicating, including phone calls to friends, text messages to friends, anything electronic from her computer to her friends' computers. Well, not everything. The Brown family has a computer in their living room for Zach, Jennifer, and John to use. Mr. Brown or Ms. Brown has to be in the living room for the computer to be used. There is just too much junk on the Internet and so much potential for abusive, illegal activity through the Internet that limits are necessary.

Jennifer had put her clothes out last night. She does not like to select her clothes in the morning, because she is not completely alert then. In the social priorities of Jennifer and her friends, fashion mistakes are just not allowed.

Jennifer is ready to go to school, and her brother John is heading out the door. John is willing to take Jennifer to school because Mr. Brown and Ms. Brown made that a condition of John getting a car before his senior year of high school. As usual, Jennifer has a question for her older brother as they drive to her middle school.

"Hey, John, a counselor from your high school spoke to the eighth graders at our school last week. She told us all about classes and clubs and stuff. She said that she would be back in a month or two so we could sign up for classes and fill out some survey. The classes look okay, but what clubs and stuff should I get involved in?"

John is an expert on high school clubs, sports, and similar activities. He has been involved in high school extracurricular activities. "Well, don't do everything I did just because I did it, but the best high school group I've been part of is the marching band. It is tons of work. Those band contests are not easy. Your practices in summer are long and hot, but you get to take neat trips later. We got invited to play at a college football game last year and that was great. It costs a lot of money to get band uniforms and instruments, so you have to help with fund-raising events. There is nothing free in marching band. There are no credit cards, either. All students have to account for money they raise by selling stuff or working at the huge yard sale or, you know, everything else school groups do to make money.

"I like tennis and I've played on the tennis team every year. I even played on the high school tennis team in the spring when I was in eighth grade. That gets you involved in high school early.

"Oh, yeah. The student technology club is great. We actually get paid to do some computer work at school in the summer. I worked at school last summer for 3 weeks and I made $10 an hour. I still do some computer work for the school and they have this deal with a local business. After I do 50 hours of work this school year, I get a free laptop computer when I graduate so I can use it at college."

Jennifer was impressed. "That sounds great. Thanks for the ideas. Hey, we're already at my school. Thanks, for the ride, John. See you tonight."

Jennifer was gone before John could reply to her. What motivated her eager entrance into her middle school? You guessed it—friends. Each day at school, Jennifer and her best friends sat together in the cafeteria, where everyone waited until it was time to go to their lockers and then to first-period class. Today, Andrea, Christie, and Whitney were at the table when Jennifer arrived. Whitney told Jennifer the latest news.

"Jennifer, it's so cool. Listen to this. Andrea and Christie are going to start doing the morning TV news show here at school. Next month they will be the anchor team reading the news. I'm going to do the weather report. We asked Ms. Harvey—she organizes the news program—and she said you could do a daily sports report. You play a lot of tennis, right? So sports would be great for you. Here's the best part. During our month we get to sell commercials. You know, businesses buy time on our news show to advertise their products. The school gets half of the money to help pay for field trips. The other half goes to a club at school that the news crew picks. We were thinking maybe the French Club or the student council. What do you think?"

Jennifer thought for a moment. "This is great. We get to be on TV at school. We get to make money. How about that food drive project? We could donate money to help get more food. I think the student council is organizing the food drive."

Andrea agreed. "Perfect. They always need more food. It's really sad that some people are hungry. Hey, did you hear about Bruce and Anthony? They got in trouble at school yesterday in the bus area or on the bus or something. They have to come to school on Saturday and clean the building."

Christie changed the topic. "Is anybody going to that concert next month? The tickets cost so much, but that band is the best. The cheapest ticket is $40. My mother would never pay that much for me to go."

"Yeah, I'm going," Jennifer said. "My brother knows somebody who works at the concert arena. He said they give tickets to about 20 people who stay after the concert and help clean the place for 2 hours. It actually makes money for the high school marching band. Twenty students help clean the place. They get great tickets free. The marching band gets $400. It's great for everyone. Maybe we can do that when we are in high school."

Andrea got everyone's attention. "Look. There's Ms. Harvey. Let's go talk to her about the news."

Christie was up instantly. Jennifer and Whitney were right behind her. The girls talked to Ms. Harvey for a minute and then the bell rang. That is the signal for everyone to go to lockers and then report to first-period class in 7 minutes.

The morning classes were fine for Jennifer—nothing great, nothing awful, just pretty much regular classroom activities of books and worksheets plus a quiz and one video. The best part of the day was coming up soon. Halfway through math class was the 29-minute break for lunch. Jennifer was never all that hungry at lunch, but she ate a regular meal. What made lunch great was friends. Jennifer had done all of the required work in her classes during the morning. She turned in all homework. She paid attention. She took notes. She knew everything on the quiz. She is a successful student. Still, no class at school gets the same eager excitement from Jennifer as does a conversation with her friends. Some of Jennifer's best friends are in her math class, so they get to go to lunch together. Students are required to not talk in the hallways going to and from lunch because other classes are in session, but once in the cafeteria, they can begin their conversations.

"I saw them together this morning before first-period class. I think he really likes her, but she, you know, she's just waiting for her old boyfriend to get jealous so they can get back together." Whitney kept everyone informed about the latest social news.

Andrea had another topic on her mind. "Hey, are any of you going to the tryouts for the school play? Our school has never had a real play, but the new seventh-grade language arts teacher is going to sponsor it. I think it would be so neat to do that. Tryouts are tomorrow after school. Who wants to go with me?"

Jennifer and Christie both said "I do" immediately. This group of best friends liked to do school activities together, and each had plenty of outgoing personality to impress any judge at a theatrical tryout.

Jennifer was glad that tryouts were tomorrow, not today. "I have to leave school early today to go to the orthodontist. I'll get these braces off in 6 or 7 months. Today I guess they will tighten the wires and stuff. That always hurts, but I'll still go to the play tryouts tomorrow."

Their conversation continued until it was time to return to math class. The 1:00 bell ended math and all other classes. The halls were full of active, busy, talkative middle school students. Jennifer went to her locker to get the U.S. history book she needed for her next class and to get everything else she would need to take with her so she could leave on time at 2:00, which was toward the end of her history class.

U.S. history class began differently today. The lights were turned off. There was some type of music playing softly. The teacher then started showing a collection of photographs from the Civil War. These pictures were projected on the screen in the front of the room from a new computer-connected projection system. The teacher then recited word for exact word President Abraham Lincoln's Gettysburg Address. Jennifer was impressed. The entire class was captivated. The closing words of the speech were followed by spontaneous applause from 27 very intrigued eighth graders. The class discussion that followed was fascinating. The teacher stayed in character as President Lincoln and answered questions from students as if they were all back in the Civil War years. Jennifer had never been so amazed with history. She was actually sorry when it was time for her to leave class and leave school early. She got to the office at 2:00 and her mother was there, ready to take her to the orthodontist. Mom had asked for and just received a copy of Jennifer's most recent report card because their orthodontist gave students a $20 discount on the monthly office visit when you showed a current report card with all grades of A and B. Jennifer always qualified for the discount, so her parents split the savings with her. That gave Jennifer an extra $10 per month deposited into her savings account.

Ms. Brown and Jennifer talked about Ms. Brown's business trip to the book-publishing conference. Ms. Brown is working on a new series of character education books for children. Jennifer suggested making the Gettysburg Address into a book about history so children could understand the Civil War. Ms. Brown was intrigued by the possibility of history books for children, and while Jennifer was in the orthodontist's chair, Ms. Brown e-mailed that idea to her publisher. Jennifer was thrilled that her idea was being taken so seriously.

After the orthodontist work was completed, Jennifer and her mother stopped at the grocery store. Milk, cereal, bananas, coffee, fruit juice, bread, and ice cream were on their list. Then they stopped at a gasoline station. The price of gas was up again and Ms. Brown said to Jennifer, "Honey, when you start driving in a few years, I'm afraid gas will be much more expensive. Our next car will have to get better mileage than this one. Maybe we should get a hybrid."

"We studied those in science class and in math class," Jennifer replied. "They get great mileage, but they cost more than regular cars. Still, some people end up saving money with them."

At home that night everyone gathered for supper. Mom and Jennifer told everyone about the business trip and the orthodontist visit. Dad and Zach talked about the television station trip. John told everyone that he was now the top-rated student technology assistant at school. Now, he gets $11 per hour for the after-school technology work he does, instead of $10 an hour. After supper, Zach, Jennifer, and John had homework to do. Mr. Brown and Ms. Brown discussed that idea of U.S. history books for children and then did some chores around the house.

Jennifer finished her homework and began doing an extra credit project for U.S. history. She began memorizing the Gettysburg Address. The teacher said that any student who could recite that speech from memory would get 50 extra credit points and an automatic A on the next test. The teacher said that years ago it was rather common for eighth graders to memorize poems, quotes, or even a speech. Jennifer accepted the challenge and the opportunity.

With her father's approval and supervision, Jennifer sent a few e-mails to friends. The topics were school, the orthodontist, trying out for the school play tomorrow, and whether anything was going on this weekend. Jennifer then recited the first paragraph of the Gettysburg Address while her father listened. He was impressed with his studious daughter.

She was impressed with her wise father, who then recited the first paragraph of the Gettysburg Address.

"How did you do that, Dad? You know it word-for-word."

"We had to memorize it in eighth grade. It's been in my brain all these years. Someday you can impress your children when you recite it for them. And I'll amaze my grandchildren when I recite it with you. Time for bed now, Jennifer. Sleep well. See you in the morning. Good night, sweetheart."

Table 7.1 reviews Jennifer's day as it matches the research survey list of the essentials for understanding economics and money management success.

An extreme economics teacher can also connect the events of Jennifer's day with the basic, fundamental vocabulary of economics. Think, please, of connections between the activities Jennifer experienced on this day and how those can connect with the 17 economics terms used before. The list of terms is provided, but the list of connections is for you to complete. Learning, including learning as a book is read, is best when it is interactive and participatory.

Economics vocabulary	Connections with Jennifer
1. Law of supply and demand	
2. Production	
3. Distribution	
4. Consumption	
5. Productivity	
6. Technology	
7. Competition	
8. Specialize	
9. Money	
10. Scarcity	
11. Profit	
12. Land, labor, capital	
13. Risk	
14. Opportunity cost	
15. Interdependent	
16. Advertisement	
17. Finances	

Table 7.1. Jennifer's Day as It Matches the Research Survey List of the Essentials for Understanding Economics and Money Management Success

Research Findings	*Connections With Jennifer*
1. Save, save more, keep saving	The $20 savings at the orthodontist for good grades earns Jennifer a $10 savings account deposit.
2. Start saving now	Jennifer has a savings account.
3. Have a money plan	Making good grades is important for many reasons, including it is part of Jennifer's money plan to earn $10 extra each month.
4. Credit is deceptive	John explained that part of being in the marching band is helping raise money for the band. No credit is given or accepted. Work that makes money is accepted.
5. Live within your means	Jennifer and her mother discussed the increasing price of gasoline and the impact that will have when Jennifer is old enough to drive and share the costs of a car.
6. Life is not about money	Jennifer's day revolved around people. The money parts of her day were managed wisely, which helped the other parts go better.
7. The measurement of economics is math	Grades of A or of B are measured by numbers. Jennifer's grades met those standards so she earned the $20 monthly discount at the orthodontist.
8. Get the best and the most education	Jennifer accepted the extra challenge and the extra opportunity to memorize the Gettysburg Address.
9. Develop a strong work ethic	Trying out for the school play is extra work and being in the play would be much more work, but Jennifer expects herself to do more and be more.
10. People are more important than money	Ms. Brown confirmed this for Jennifer when she e-mailed Jennifer's idea to her publisher. Mr. Brown confirmed this as he interacted with Jennifer about the Gettysburg Address. Jennifer and her friends display this every day!

Jennifer's friendships with several students in her eighth-grade classes are important to her. She interacts cordially with most people her age and with adults. She is developing effective people skills, which can be useful to her now as a student and throughout her life, including in her career.

The following extreme economics activities have been successful with eighth graders whom I have taught in recent years. Sometimes, a student will ask if working with another student is allowed. The answer is usually yes, but students know that they will need to convince me that each partner participated fully. Some businesses are started by two business partners, so class projects or homework projects can be examples of the partnership structure of a business. This is another way to develop people skills and to build on the reality that many middle school students value friendships; so, put those alliances to work in the classroom, with friends becoming business partners.

The following classroom activities and homework projects have worked well with my students. These are presented as catalysts for creativity, so make adjustments or create newly inspired ideas so the activities and projects you design for your students reflect their life experiences and their wholesome knowledge, interests, and talents.

ACTIVITY 1

Option 1

1. Invent
    a. the grocery store of the future, or
    b. the amusement park of the future, or
    c. the car dealership of the future, or
    d. the restaurant of the future, or
    e. (your idea, which you discuss in advance with your teacher).
2. Include
    a. the name of the new business;
    b. three reasons why this is a great name;
    c. a full-page, four-color newspaper ad about the new business;
    d. a full-size, multicolor website about the new business;
    e. a drawing of the new business; and
    f. a letter, which includes a coupon about a promotional offer, both of which would be mailed to consumers, convincing them to visit your new business and make a purchase.

Option 2

1. Create a new magazine about a wholesome topic that is important to you—something you know about, are talented in, or are interested in. Discuss the topic with your teacher before you start work.

2. Include
   a. the front cover—show the name and use two or more colors;
   b. the back cover—an advertisement with two or more colors;
   c. an advertisement inside the front cover;
   d. an advertisement inside the back cover;
   e. a table of contents;
   f. four articles with a picture in each article; and
   g. a pop-out card that encourages people to subscribe to the magazine.

ACTIVITY 2

1. Create a new
   a. mega computer and electronics store, or
   b. mega sporting goods store, or
   c. mega food court in a mall, or
   d. mega automobile dealership.
2. Explain the following about the new business that you create:
   a. The idea/concept
   b. How your idea/concept is better than current places with which you will compete
3. Show the floor plan with details.
   a. Reasons for the floor plan to be as you designed it
   b. Advantages of this floor plan versus current competition
4. Draw and write a print ad for your new business.
5. Write a radio ad for your business.
6. Write a television ad, including information about video, plus the audio text, for your new business.
7. Create the first page of the website, give the website address, list the links and the 800 number.
8. Create a promotion to get people to come to your new business and to return to the business a second time.
9. Extra credit:
   a. List five reasons why people should buy stock in your new company 8 years from now, after you have opened a total of 28 locations and decide to go public.
   b. Much more extra credit: Do all of the above items, 2–8, for more than one new business.

ACTIVITY 3

Option 1

1. Create a 1- to 2-minute presentation and a 30-second commercial about the high school you are going to attend. Turn in the script of the presentation and the script of the commercial.
2. Include the following information:
   a. Location
   b. Something about the history of the school
   c. What you think is the best quality of the school
   d. Information from the school's website
   e. A quote from a person who works now at the school
   f. A quote from a student who currently attends the school

Option 2

1. Create a 1- to 2-minute presentation and a 30-second commercial about a college you are interested in attending. Turn in the script of the presentation and the script of the commercial.
2. Include the following information:
   a. Location
   b. Something about the history of the school
   c. What you think is the best quality of the school
   d. Information from the school's website
   e. A quote from a person who works now at the school, a quote from a student who currently attends the school, or a quote from a person who is a graduate of the school

Select and complete one of the following choices. Yes, you may do more than is required. Yes, you may turn this in early—be sure it is done completely and done correctly. Everything you do for this homework must be G-rated, legal, and ethical.

ACTIVITY 4

1. Select five different product categories—for example, breakfast cereal is one product category.

a. In each of the five categories, select two products—one is a well-known name brand and the other is the store brand. Tell what the two products are in each category.
b. Compare and contrast the two products in each category: the package, the price, the ingredients, the claims made, if any (e.g., "Gets the toughest dirt out"), and other important factors that you notice.
c. Tell which of the two products in each category you would buy or recommend, and give two reasons why for each.
d. Put yourself in the job of brand manager for one of the name-brand products. You are getting concerned that the store brands are taking more and more of your business. In two paragraphs or more, explain how you will compete to get your sales to increase and to get customers to return to your brand.
e. On November 16, 2005, a grocery store charged $3.45 for a box of 12 name-brand granola bars, 2 bars in each of 6 packs in the box. The store's brand of 12 granola bars was priced at $2.50 regularly but was on sale—3 for $5.00. Write the 30-second commercial appealing to customers who like granola bars to try the store's brand or to stay with the national brand name product.

2. Think of ways that eighth graders could make money during the next three months—safe, smart, realistic, practical, proper ways to make money. List at least five ways. Now, think of ways that you and another eighth grader could team up so that each of you makes more money than if you were each just working alone. List at least five ways. Now, fast-forward to March 2, 2006, and you have earned $400. You saved $300 of it. The other $100 was spent during holidays and weekends. Write a summary of everything that you did on your own and that you did with your business partner to make your $400. Use the 17 core content terms in your summary and underline each term the first time you use it.

   For one of the ways you made money, you designed and distributed a one-page advertisement that you mailed to people and handed out to people. Show the detailed design of your one-page advertisement, including all information a potential customer would need to know.

3. This option deals with the question, Which is more important to customers—the product they buy or the service that the business provides? For example, is the quality of the TV you buy at a store more

important or was the service—how you were treated, the phone call to make sure your TV was working well, the guarantee to make any repairs free for 1 year—more important?

You decide to open a lemonade stand on a hot summer Saturday in July while you are also having a family garage sale. Think of five problems related to your products and five more problems related to customer service that could happen, and tell how you will prevent those or deal with those.

4. For the next week, keep a detailed record of every possible time, place, and way that you could save, save more, and keep saving. Keep the record of who, what, when, where, and how. A list or a chart will be fine. Then put some of those ideas and other information into a four-page minimagazine that is all about saving. The minimagazine is directed toward middle school students. The information in the mini-magazine will tell students how to save, why to save, what to avoid so money is not wasted, what to watch out for that could have caused money to be spent unnecessarily. Give the minimagazine an attractive, informative cover. Name the magazine. Put an ad on the back cover. Between the covers will be four pages of information, articles, and two pictures (draw, newspaper, news magazine, print from computer), and an advice/question-and-answer column could be included. Use the following outline for one article.

   First, the year is 2009, and you are a junior in high school. You complete an application for a job at a grocery store. First, write five questions you expect to be asked, and write your very convincing, very impressive answer to each question. Your goal is to get hired.

   1.
   2.
   3.
   4.
   5.

   Second, design the store. Show the interior and the exterior. What is the name of the store? What makes this store better than other grocery stores—list three reasons your store is better than other grocery stores.

   1.
   2.
   3.

Third, when you graduate from high school, the grocery store owners say that they will help pay for your college education if you continue to work for the store 15 hours each week during college. Think of and list three reasons why the store is making you this offer.

1.
2.
3.

5. The time is February 2010 and you are being interviewed by a committee at a college or university. The committee will select the 20 high school seniors who will be given a scholarship that pays for tuition completely. That would be $8,000 to $20,000 or more per year based on current prices. Think of everything that you have accomplished during your high school years that will convince the committee to select you as 1 of the 20 scholarship winners. Now, list six questions the committee will ask you and write a one-paragraph answer for each question.

   The committee selects you for one of the scholarships. To maintain the scholarship for 4 years of college, you must make great grades and be involved in service activities. Explain how you will make great grades—tell your plan in three paragraphs. What service can you provide to the school? Explain this in two paragraphs.
6. Save. Save more. Keep saving. You enter a contest to create advertisements that communicate the ideas of Save. Save more. Keep saving. Create each of the following:
   a. A 30-second radio commercial—time it to be sure of length
   b. A 30-second television commercial—time it to be sure of length
   c. A website—homepage with five link boxes
   d. A one-half-page newspaper ad
   e. A bumper sticker
   f. A T-shirt
7. Invent the ultimate fitness facility. From training for sports to getting back into shape, this is the perfect place.
   a. Name: Give three reasons why it is a great name
   b. Website: Design homepage and indicate six links.
   c. A 30-second radio commercial: Write the script.
   d. Promotion event: What will happen at the grand opening?
   e. Special trial offer: Create the quarter-page ad in the newspaper and the coupon that is included.

f. Special offer: Get people who visit as a guest to return and join.
g. Membership prices: Determine the levels of various memberships.

ACTIVITY 5

From the following descriptions, design a business that matches Description 1 or 2, your choice. You will present a 3- to 5-minute infomercial in class about the business.

1. It's big. Really, really big. It is the ultimate sports, activity, recreation facility. It has all of the following activities with fields, indoor courts . . . everything:
   Softball fields
   Swimming pools
   Basketball courts
   Dancing studio and dancing floor
   Soccer—indoor fields and outdoor fields
   Tennis courts—indoor and outdoor
   Volleyball—indoor court and outdoor sand-filled area
   Hockey—roller-hockey and ice hockey
   Skateboarding—indoor and outdoor ramps and more
   Football—flag football indoors and football fields outside
   Baseball—batting cage indoors and fields outdoors

   These are leagues, pick-up games, lessons, camps, and much more. Sure, we also have a gigantic concession cafeteria, a snack area, a coffee area, and a sporting goods store.
2. Everything creative you can think of, you'll find it here. Movies to watch in very comfortable theaters. Every type of proper video game and every type of video game system. Internet access. Music and music and music, including live bands. Art, crafts, and skills classes to learn about singing, modeling, sculpture, pottery, writing, dancing, and more. A library of books, magazines, and endless employment information from places you could get a job and endless applications for colleges, universities, and vocational/technical schools. A food court complete with Starbucks. Plus, singing competitions with great prizes on Friday night and on Saturday afternoon and night.

ACTIVITY 6

Select one of the following:

1. Invent a product that is G-rated, legal, and ethical. It might be a new snack—think of your favorite snack and invent a better version of that. It might be a new high-technology gadget. Maybe you are interested in fashion and you design new clothing styles. Include the following:
   a. The name of your new product and two reasons why that is the perfect name
   b. At least three ways that your product is better than its competition
   c. The package the new product comes in—design the package and make a sample/prototype of the package
   d. The homepage of the website of the new product—show six links
   e. A quarter-page newspaper ad or a 30-second radio ad or a 30-second TV ad for the new product
2. Invent a new store/business that is G-rated, legal, and ethical—such as a clothing store, a grocery store, a sports equipment store, a movie theater, a restaurant—and come up with the following:
   a. The name of the store/business and two reasons why that is the perfect name
   b. At least three ways that your store/business is better than its competition
   c. The exterior design of the new store/business and the interior design/floor plan of the new store/business
   d. The homepage of the website of the new store—show six links
   e. A quarter-page newspaper ad or a 30-second radio ad or a 30-second TV ad for the new store/business

We now visit John to explore his day as a high school student and the many possible connections with economics and John's real life.

8

A DAY IN THE ECONOMIC LIFE OF A HIGH SCHOOL STUDENT

The senior year of high school is a busy, wonderful, demanding, exciting, frustrating, lively time for Jason Jonathan Brown, who has always gone by John. In his kindergarten class there were four boys named Jason. It was very confusing. John had sometimes been called J. J. or Double-J or Jonathan while he was young, but for some reason he always liked being called John. He said it might be because both of his grandfathers were named John. The kindergarten-name situation was the perfect reason to make it official, so it has been that way for 12 years—John.

College. College. College. If any one topic seemed to dominate John's senior year of high school, it was college. An admissions representative from a different college or university visited John's high school every day during the first semester. Their presentations were always personal, professional, and persuasive. John attended a few of these presentations, but he had already applied to five colleges fairly early in his senior year. His goal was to have all of that process completed by December 1 of the senior year so he could get it off his mind before the final exam week ended the first semester in mid-December.

Money. Money. Money. John was concluding that college was more about money than it was about classes or a degree. No matter what else anyone said about a college or a university, the reality was always how to pay for it. John's 3.85 grade point average placed him in the top 10% of his senior class. He had taken several advanced placement classes as a junior and was taking three more during his senior year. He also had two dual-credit classes, which were taught at his high school by instructors from a nearby college. The two classes count toward high school graduation and earn college credit. John's senior year of high school was his busiest, but he planned it that way. He saw no reason to relax this year and then get shocked by the difficulties of the first year of college.

John's skills in technology earned an upgraded $11-per-hour job for him at his school. He works at school 2 days each week, from about 4:30 until 5:00 or 5:30 doing computer work. He can repair computers. He can fix wiring. He can install anything. The school's technology director works around John's marching-band schedule so the marching band practices and the technology work schedule fit well.

John's technology job income goes into his savings account. His parents are going to help with college tuition costs, but with scholarships John earns—he has applied for many scholarships from every possible source; writing those essays and completing those applications get old, but 6 hours of writing might become a $1,000 per year scholarship and that is a great hourly wage—they hope to be able to pay for the remaining costs of tuition, room, and board. John will pay for his books. He estimates $1,000 per year for college books, so his savings account gets all he can put in it.

If you ask John what he likes best about high school, he will give you a polite, diplomatic, yet honest and genuine answer. "I like my classes. They are hard, but that will get me ready for college. I like my part-time job at school. Technology is so cool, and I get paid for doing computer stuff that I like to do anyway. You asked me what I liked best about high school. That's easy. Friday nights during the football season, I get to help in the press box with the statistics of the game and with operating the scoreboard. Then at halftime I get to march with the band. After the game I update the school's website with the sports statistics. One parent who helps in the press box heard about the website work I do after each game. His advertising company might want to hire me next summer to help them with advertising on the Internet and with updating websites for some of their clients. He's going to pay for me to take some really advanced computer training so I have the right qualifications. If I do all of that, I can pay for college books and still save a lot of money. Oh, yeah, my girlfriend is in the band. So that makes Friday nights even better. Her name is Kim. She writes sports stories for our high school newspaper so she uses all of those sports statistics I put on the school website. So, all of that is what I like best about high school."

The school day for John gets off to a fast start. After he takes Jennifer to middle school, he goes directly to high school, hoping to get a parking space. There are more student drivers than there are spaces in the student parking lots. John was selected as student of the week once during his junior year, and the reward was a reserved parking space for a week. He hopes to earn that again one week during his senior year. John would like a newer car, but he is glad to have any car that drives. He and his parents set up a budget when John was 16 years old and earned his driver's license. Only a used car fit in the budget. John promises himself a newer car someday, but for now a 7-year-old car with 86,000 miles on it is fine.

With three advanced placement classes, two dual-credit classes, and one elective class, John's class schedule is full. His parents insisted that he take a serious schedule of classes during his senior year rather than just do enough to get by. They were concerned that an easy senior year of high school could lead to a difficult freshman year of college.

John's three advanced placement classes are in the morning. His brain gets a thorough workout during that advanced placement triple play. His next class is the band elective class, and this extended period includes 30 minutes for lunch. At lunch John usually eats with several friends from band. Today, his good friends Shawn and Tasha sit with John at lunch. Once a week during marching season, the marching band practices before school starts, early in the morning. They have some after-school practices each week during marching season. Band class is music history, music theory, biographies of great musicians, specific work by instrument sections, and full band rehearsal. It is demanding work but John, Tasha, Shawn, and the other students in the marching band are dedicated to the work, the music, the band director, and each other.

Tasha sounded excited and a little anxious. "Friday night's football game will be great. Both teams are undefeated. Our band will march right after the other school's band marches. It's like a one-on-one band competition. Then we leave early Saturday morning for the huge band competition. I read the website of this band competition. There will be something like 48 bands competing at four different football fields. Then the top 2 bands from each location have a final competition Saturday night. I can't wait."

Shawn was just as excited. "My dad told me that next year our school is going to host a band competition. He said they can make a lot of money from ticket tales, concession sales, and the printed program. He wants his company to be the big sponsor of the event."

John changed the subject. "Do you guys have a lot of tests this week? I'm excited about the band stuff, but I have four big tests this week. I have after-school technology work to do. We had two band practices after school this week. Maybe college will actually be easier than high school."

Shawn was pessimistic. "Not from what I hear. Freshman year is tough. That's when some college students quit or flunk out. My mother is always asking me about my college applications and my scholarship applications. I did some online. The others are just forms to fill out and essays to write. My essays were about working last summer in the movie theater. I got promoted to assistant manager. I thought colleges would be impressed that my employer promoted me, plus I went to that entrepreneur conference and we created a complete business plan for a new store we created. That will help me get in a good college."

Tasha wondered, "You still have to get great test scores and have great grades. Are you taking that college test again or have you already done that, Shawn?"

"Did it last summer. My score was much better. This time I understood how that test was set up. When I took it last year, I did nothing to prepare. This time I really practiced a lot with sample tests."

John had to leave lunch early. "Listen, I have to go. Kim and I are doing some work in the library. We both have huge research projects due next month. She's already in the library getting information about the Declaration of Independence. My topic is the Bill of Rights. This advanced placement government class is harder than I expected."

"You can do it, John. Just remember how much easier college will be. Oh, my fault, college is going to be harder, isn't it? Well, do the work now anyway; maybe everything just gets more complicated. See you later." Shawn smiled and John forced a grin as he wondered if everything would always be more demanding and more complicated.

John had about 10 minutes to work in the library. Kim was searching U.S. history–related websites and found an abundance of materials about the Declaration of Independence. John searched the Internet and found more Bill of Rights information than he would need for five papers. That gave him the idea to use the Bill of Rights topic for all research or other writing projects during the rest of his senior year.

The afternoon classes were the dual-credit courses John was taking for simultaneous high school credit and college credit. One class was taught by an instructor who was completing his doctorate in sociology at a nearby university. The other dual-credit class was introduction to American novels and was taught by a teacher who taught for 30 years at John's high school, then completed her doctorate and now taught part-time.

When school ended for the day, John checked his cell phone for e-mail messages. Mom was home from her trip; she e-mailed and was getting Jennifer at school early to go to the orthodontist. Dad had picked up Zach, and they were going to the TV station. John thought of his years of wearing braces and of visits he had to the TV station. Great memories, but there was work to do now. John had an hour or so of technology work to do for the school. He had tons of homework, including all of those tests to study for. About 4:30, he drove home and then organized everything he would need to do the rest of the day and night. He joined his family for supper, heard the stories everyone had to tell about their day, and added his report about the busy marching-band schedule.

John's parents checked in with him once or twice during the evening. They both expressed their pride in his serious approach to studying, band, his technology job, and the sports statistics work. Mom brought him a snack about 8:30 and Dad brought him a book about the how the first amendment in the Bill of Rights affects television news reporting. John finished his work at 10:30 and sent Kim a friendly e-mail from the family computer, as his parents smiled their approval. Dad made a mental note to send his wife a friendly e-mail tomorrow during the day. John had given Dad a good idea. Sometimes, a parent or guardian can learn from a child or teenager. John then went to sleep so he could be ready for tomorrow's challenges and opportunities.

If you are teaching John during his senior year of high school, you have the life experiences of 17 or 18 years that John brings with him to the classroom every day. He also brings an impressive collection of wholesome knowledge, interests, and talents. Using just what is known from this day in the life of a high school senior, how could the experiences of this one day relate to the research survey and to the vocabulary of economics?

The vocabulary of economics was not heard in John's conversations or pointed out during his activities, but an extreme economics teacher could certainly connect that vocabulary with the real life that John is living. Please complete the following list. One connection per vocabulary term is given, but please add another connection from the day in the life of John or from a day in the life of another high school student whom you know or teach.

Table 8.1. Vocabulary of Economics and Connections With John

Research Findings	*Connections With John*
1 Save, save more, keep saving	1. John has a savings account to pay for college books.
2. Start saving now	2. Despite temptations to spend now, John is saving for future college costs.
3. Have a money plan	3. John and his parents have divided the college costs in an established plan.
4. Credit is deceptive	4. John will have the cash saved for college books. He will not use a credit card to buy these and begin college $500 in debt.
5. Live within your means	5. John drives a used car because that fits in the budget.
6. Life is not about money	6. Family, friends, girlfriend, school classes, school activities. and college plans are priorities for John.
7. The measurement of economics is math	7. John's good work in his technology job earned a raise from $10 per hour to $11 per hour.
8. Get the best and the most	8. John is taking advanced placement classes, education dual-credit classes, and technology training/certification.
9. Develop a strong work ethic	9. John manages his time to do the technology work, study for tests, and read for a research paper.
10. People are more important than money	10. John takes his sister to school. John visits with friends at lunch. John spends time with his family at home.

Table 8.2. Vocabulary of Economics and Connections with John

Economic Vocabulary	*Connections With John*
1. Law of supply and demand	a. Tests to study for and a paper to write were demands on John's limited supply of time. b.
2. Production	a. John is responsible for producing/making his research report on the Bill of Rights. b.
3. Distribution	a. The e-mail to Kim was distributed via the Internet. b.
4. Consumption	a. Lunch was consumed. b.
5. Productivity	a. The demands of this week require that John gets more done, so he budgets his time well and eliminates some other possible uses of time. b.
6. Technology	a. His job after school is as a technology expert. b.
7. Competition	a. Marching-band contests are held with many high school bands involved. b.
8. Specialize	a. His idea was to continue the Bill of Rights as a research topic for many projects during his senior year of high school. b.
9. Money	a. John has anticipated the costs of college. b.
10. Scarcity	a. There was not enough money to buy a new car, so John drives the used car. b.
11. Profit	a. The high school's hosting a marching band competition can make money. b.
12. Land, labor, capital	a. Earth, work, and money are required for a marching band competition. b.
13. Risk	a. Will colleges that John applies to accept him as a student or not? b.
14. Opportunity cost	a. After being accepted at several colleges, John will attend only one—saying yes to one means saying no to the others. b.
15. Interdependent	a. Everyone in John's family is helpful. b.
16. Advertisement	a. All of the college representatives who visited John's school gave students a lot of printed material to advertise the college. b.
17. Finances	a. This involved applying for and getting as many college scholarships as possible. b.

Some high school seniors have shopped for a car, applied for and held part-time jobs, been responsible for buying their own clothes, done all of the budgeting for future college costs, and had other direct and real encounters with economics. Those same high school seniors still enjoy simpler parts of life, such as candy bars, magazines, stores/malls, and movies. The following classroom activities are additional catalysts for creativity, so please read them and then create extreme economics classroom activities based on the life experiences of your students and their wholesome knowledge, interests, and talents.

Here is another source of ideas. The days in the lives of Zach, Jennifer, and John presented here concentrate on events during school days. Consider life experiences of your students on weekends and during the summer as additional sources of extreme economics connections. Then take the time to trade your extreme ideas with other teachers. Students would be fascinated to see all of their subjects at school taught with a continual connection to their life experiences and to their wholesome knowledge, talents, and interests. Some connection activity ideas for extreme economics follow.

Remember when we took the survey to identify what your favorite snack is and what your favorite candy bar is? Well, now you get to think about and create the ultimate snack or candy bar.

Your choice: Create a new candy bar or create a new snack.

1. Name this product and give four reasons why it is a good name.
2. In writing and in drawing, describe the taste, the shape, the texture, and the size of the snack or candy bar.
3. Create the package or draw a picture of the package it comes in (if drawn, show all sides).
4. Draw and write an advertisement for the new product.

"New, from Super Candy Concepts, the first variety of candy bars that come with a variety of dipping candy sauces. You like chocolate, don't you? You like lots of other flavors, too. Well, up until now, no other candy could give you every flavor you want, whenever you want it, but new Rainbow Yummies are the candies you have always wanted.

"Here's how it works. You begin with a perfectly delicious bar of chocolate, vanilla, or strawberry candy. What's even better, this is a big portion of candy. Now, you take your big candy bar of chocolate or vanilla or strawberry and you dip it into one of the sauces that come in oblong tubs. Sauce flavors include 'extreme chocolate,' 'lively lemon,' 'biggest blueberry,' 'cool cookie dough,' 'colorful cotton candy,' 'wonderful watermelon,' 'perfect peanut butter,' 'crunchy peanuts,' and 'magical marshmallow.' A different dipping sauce in an oblong tub comes with each Rainbow Yummies candy bar you buy.

"Rainbow Yummies can be purchased in single packages with only a chocolate candy bar, with only a vanilla candy bar, or with only a strawberry bandy bar, so you can get your favorite flavor. You could buy the variety triple package, which has one each of the chocolate, vanilla, and strawberry candy bars. Of course, with each purchase of a Rainbow Yummies candy bar, you get one tub of dipping sauce! The variety triple pack comes with three dipping sauces! Rainbow Yummies are also available in bite-size portions, which come in a package of 36 pieces, with 12 chocolate pieces, 12 vanilla pieces, and 12 strawberry pieces, plus six different dipping sauce tubs.

"So, what are you waiting for? Look, there's a rainbow. Well, actually it is Rainbow Yummies candy as far as the eye can see. Be sure to enter our Draw a Rainbow Contest. You could win a year's supply of Rainbow Yummies if you draw the rainbow scene that looks most like Rainbow Yummies candy."

Part 1: Now, using the following list explain how Rainbow Yummies relate to these 17 economic core content concepts. Give your answer in the column to the right of the terms.

Economic concept	Rainbow Yummies
1. Interdependent	
2. Land, labor, capital	
3. Scarcity	
4. Advertisements	
5. Finance	
6. Opportunity cost	

7. Profit
8. Risk
9. Law of supply and demand
10. Money
11. Competition
12. Production
13. Distribution
14. Consumption
15. Productivity
16. Technology
17. Specialize

Part 2: Answer this candy math question.

The single Rainbow Yummies candy bar and 1 dipping sauce costs 59 cents.

The variety pack of 3 Rainbow Yummies candy bars and 3 dipping sauces costs $1.49.

The big variety bag of 36 bite-size pieces and 6 dipping sauces costs $2.49, and 6 bite-size pieces equals 1 full-size Rainbow Yummies candy bar.

So, based on money and math, which is the best deal: the single candy bar, the variety pack of candy bars, or the variety bag of bite-size pieces? Show your math and explain your reasons for your answer.

Part 3: Improvements.

1. Think of a better name for this new candy than Rainbow Yummies and give three reasons why your new name is better.
   New name:
   Three reasons why it is better:
   a.
   b.
   c.
2. Think of three improvements that could be made in the Rainbow Yummies candy bars and dipping sauces and tell why you think consumers would like the three changes.

Improvements	Why consumers would like the changes:
a.	a.
b.	b.
c.	c.

3. Think of and list three products other than the original Rainbow Yummies candy with dipping sauce that could expand the Rainbow Yummies line of products.
   a.
   b.
   c.

Freedom + ideas + capital + management + work = blended fuel of capitalism.
Note: Capitalism does not ensure success; rather, capitalism provides the opportunity for you to purse success.

"Everything chocolate, everything sweet,
Everything dessert, every yummy treat.
Cookies, cakes and pies, candy and gum
Ice cream and absolutely everything that goes yum
Fruit juice, smoothies, fresh fruit, healthy snacks, and more
Or mix up a new treat using any goodies from our store.
Everything chocolate, other flavors, and endless goodies
Plus buy one, get one free on Everything Chocolate shirts or hoodies
Please tell your friends and your family, too
Everything Chocolate is like a dessert mall, amusement park, or zoo
So, of course, we have animal crackers in many flavors and sizes
Plus everyone who comes in during June can register for free prizes.
Two great locations—one in Willtown and one in Hillside Trace
For fun and for treats, Everything Chocolate is the only place."

1. For the Everything Chocolate Shop, the menu must include the following:
   a.
   b.
   c.

   d.
   e.
   f.
2. The menu cannot include the following:
   a.
   b.
   c.
3. The interior of the shop will have this décor, style, and atmosphere:
4. To ensure that people come back for a second and third visit, what can we do?
5. When a competitor opens nearby, what can we wisely, legally, and ethically do?

You will create a magazine. The magazine will have each of the following:

1. A front cover: magazine name, cover story picture, and topic
2. An ad on the inside cover—you design the ad
3. A back cover with an ad on it—you design the ad or cut and paste
4. Inside back cover with an ad on it—you design the ad
5. Table of contents
6. Four articles: two you write and two you may cut/paste/copy, giving credit to the original source; writing all four articles is fine
7. A letter-to-the-editor page with at least two letters from readers
8. A pop-out subscription card

Topics:

1. A college you are interested in. The college website, people who have attended the college, materials you get by mail, news stories are possible sources of information.
2. A career you are interested in. People who are preparing for that career and people who are in that career, websites, materials you get from people in the career or through the mail, news stories are possible sources of information.
3. Saving and investing money. People who work for a bank or a financial company, websites, publications about money, and other news stories are possible sources of information.

Note: One of the stories/articles you write will be an interview—with eight questions you ask and eight answers you get—with someone (a) who attends/attended the college or university, (b) who is currently working in the career that interests you, or (c) who can give you ideas about how to save and how to invest based on his or her career and personal experiences.

CAR MATH

Dear ________________,

I need your advice, please. I'm thinking about buying a car. I need your thoughts about the best way to pay for it. I'll make a down payment, and I'll finance $20,000 with the car company. I might finance this over 36 months, 48 months, or 60 months. I plan to keep the car for about 8 years, so I'll get it paid off and keep it after that. What option would you advise me to take—the 3-year plan, the 4-year plan, or the 5-year plan? Please tell me the reasons for the option you prefer and the reasons for the options you advise against. Thanks for your help.

Sincerely,

____

Special deal of 1.9% interest on a car =

@ 36 monthly payments, $28.60 per $1,000 borrowed

@ 48 monthly payments, $21.65 per $1,000 borrowed

So, you have completed your plan to get into your first full-time job, and you decide to borrow $10,000 to buy a car. If your plan has you beginning graduate school, let's include the reality that you are working 20 hours weekly while you go to graduate school. Either way, you saved $3,000 and made a big down payment of $3,000 to buy the car and finance $10,000. This is the last time you will ever have to borrow money to buy a car—why?

1. How much money will your monthly payments be if you finance this for 36 months?
2. How much will you pay during the 36 months for the $10,000 you borrowed? Show the work.

3. How much money would your monthly payments be if you finance this for 48 months?
4. How much will you pay during the 48 months for the $10,000 you borrowed? Show the work.
5. "Now, if you buy this car today, we can include this package of extra accessories for only $499. The extra heavy-duty car mats and the trunk luggage holder really come in handy. Plus, this package includes the two extra sound system speakers. They all usually cost over $900, but we want to show our appreciation for your business today." What do you say to this offer—be polite, but be precise.

BUDGET

Item	Amount	Adjusted amount
Income	$48,000/year $ 4,000/month = $ 2,559/take home	
Expenses		
Mortgage, per month (as are all expenses listed)	$600 = $100,000 loan at 6% over 30 years; ($844 if over 15 years)	
Car payment	$350	
Car insurance	$70	
Home insurance	$40	
Life insurance	$50	
Car repair	$50	
Gasoline	$80	
Water bill	$25	
Utility bill	$70	
Phone—land line	$40	
Phone—cell	$40	
Cable TV and Internet	$70	
Groceries	$250	
House: maintenance, fix	$100	
IRA	$250	
Savings account	$150	

Clothes, laundry	$100
Graduate school	$100
Physician, medications	$50
Dentist	$50
Entertainment: movies, restaurants, sports	$100
Property tax	$100
Total: balanced or not	
Taxes: (deducted from paycheck monthly)	
Federal income	$700*
Social Security	$248 *
Medicare	$58*
State income tax	$240*
Local taxes	$140*
Total tax deductions:	$1,386 (total of * items)
Other deductions:	
Health insurance	$15
Dental insurance	$15
Disability insurance	$25
Total other deductions	$55
Total deductions:	
Monthly gross income:	
All deductions:	

Monthly take home (net) income =
All expenses =
Bottom line =

Conclusions:
1.
2.
3.

FUTURE BUSINESSES

1. It is the year 2016. The big retail store of 2016 has many differences versus the big retail store of 2006. Some products are new and did

not exist in 2006. Some products are still around but have changed a bit or a lot. The store looks a lot different. What people do when they go through the checkout lane is nothing like it used to be.

a. List five new products that are sold in 2016 that are not sold in 2006. Give one reason why each of these products is successful.
b. List five products that are sold in 2016 and that are sold in 2006, but tell how they have been improved in that 10-year period.
c. Draw the interior of the store, showing 10 departments, the aisles, the checkout areas, and other details.
d. Explain everything that is different about the checkout lane and the check-out process.

2. In the year 2016, people will still drive cars, trucks, and other yet-to-be invented vehicles. People will still go to car/truck dealerships to purchase cars, but the Internet may be used in more ways than it is now with the purchase of vehicles. People will be concerned with many factors, such as
   - the price of the vehicle,
   - the appearance of the vehicle,
   - how reliable the vehicle is,
   - the resale value of the vehicle,
   - the reputation of the vehicle for good performance, and
   - how long the vehicle is likely to last.

   a. Write descriptions of two different yet popular vehicles that people will buy in 2016.
   b. Draw and/or describe the dealership where these vehicles are purchased.
   c. Write a commercial for one of the new vehicles—the commercial will be broadcast during Super Bowl L (50).
   d. Think of and tell us how the vehicle could be advertised using cell phones.

9

A VISIT TO A MIDDLE SCHOOL EXTREME ECONOMICS CLASS

"Mom. Dad. I have this homework project for economics class. Its going to be a lot of work. I don't know how to get it done with everything else I have to do."

Ken and Andrea Johnson looked at each other with that knowing glance that husband and wife, father and mother, uniquely experience. Ken replied to his daughter's concern. "Well, Christie, you are right. There is a lot to do. School, piano lessons, your church youth group events, chores here at home, volleyball practices. This a very busy time already and the school year just started 2 weeks ago. Tell us more about the homework project."

Christie spoke with a bit of an eighth grader's inherent skill at drama yet with a genuine frustration that there was too much work and not enough time.

"It's actually a neat project. I mean, it's about television. I love television, but I'd rather watch TV than do a project about TV. Still, at least it's not some dumb busywork. Anyway, I have to create a new product and then create an infomercial about it. You know, one of those long TV program–type commercials that seem like a TV show but is just a long commercial."

Mom thought she had a helpful idea. "Most of the infomercials I see are for exercise equipment or for some vitamin. You are a great volleyball player, Christie. Maybe your infomercial could be for a new exercise machine designed to help volleyball players practice their skills alone. Then, between practices or when there is nobody else to practice with, a volleyball player could practice alone."

Christie was encouraged. "That would be so cool. The machine could pitch up volleyballs that you spike. It could pass the ball to you. Maybe the ball could be attached to a string or a rope that winds up in the machine so you don't have to chase it after you smash the ball. That's what I'll create. Thanks, Mom."

Dad was curious. "What will you call your new volleyball machine, Christie?"

"How about Super Smash? Maybe Smash-O-Matic. I know, Super Smash System. It's not just a little machine; it is an entire system that let's you work on every really important aspect of volleyball. How's that sound?"

"Great," Mom answered. "Now, supper is finished, so you and I have the kitchen to clean up. Your Dad is going to cut the grass. We'll be finished in the kitchen soon and you can organize your schedule for the evening. Volleyball practice today filled the time from after school until supper, so you have a busy evening, but you also have a great idea for your economics project."

Christie was confident. "I'm going to get that project done in no time. Who knows, maybe someday there will be a real infomercial for a real Super Smash System."

Christie's parents appreciated the creative homework project that their daughter had been given. Mr. Johnson and Ms. Johnson were frustrated when they had to convince Christie to do one more set of worksheets or one more page of odd-numbered problems. Sometimes, it was difficult to give Christie convincing reasons to do homework that was so ordinary, repetitious, and superficial. Occasionally, all they could say is "Well, you just have to do the work." With the infomercial assignment, Christie is eager to do the work. She is no longer concerned about being so busy or worried about having an impossible amount of work to do. She is fascinated, motivated, and determined. Her economics class project connects with her strong interest in volleyball. She is already motivated by volleyball, so that commitment carries over to the economics project. Christie is not asking, "Why do I have to do this dumb project?" or "When will I ever use this in real life?" because the project is real to her right now. To learn more about how Christie is being taught, we visit her extreme economics classroom.

"Good Tuesday afternoon, everyone. How was lunch? That's our economics class brain warm-up question today, so while I check attendance and put that report in the computer, each of you will write an evaluation of lunch. Your economics class folder should be open, your pen or pencil should be writing, your brain should be working, and your mouth is resting."

After 1 minute of silent thinking, Ms. Tammy Gray, eighth-grade economics teacher and U.S. history teacher, began the discussion. "Before you read descriptions of lunch, let's take a quick survey to see what each of you ate for lunch. Whitney, you start us, please, and then we'll go down each row. Whitney, what did you have for lunch? And then everyone else gives a quick, short answer to the same question."

"Pizza."

"Chicken nuggets."

"Chicken nuggets."

"Peanut butter and jelly sandwich."

"Pizza."

"Pizza."

"Pizza."

"A big salad."

"Chicken nuggets."

"I brought lunch. Soup and a sandwich."

"A big salad."

"Pizza."

"Chicken nuggets."

"Pizza."

"Pizza."

"A big salad."

"I brought lunch. A sandwich and some cookies and a banana."

"A turkey sandwich."

"Pizza."

"Chicken nuggets."

"Pizza."

"Pizza."

"Turkey sandwich."

"Pizza."

"Chicken nuggets."

"Very good. Now, let's get a quick count. Andrea, you were keeping track for us of the results. What did you find out?"

Andrea spoke with the confidence of a certified public accountant. That actually is her career goal, so she usually does the record keeping with any quick surveys in class, and she often helps in the class when analysis of business numbers is done. Andrea was ready with her report of the survey. "Pizza was the top choice. Eleven students had pizza for lunch. Chicken nuggets came in second, with 6 students having that for lunch. Sandwiches were next, with 2 turkey sandwiches, 2 sandwiches brought from home, and 1 peanut butter and jelly sandwich. There were 3 students who had a big salad. That's everyone except for you, Ms. Gray. What did you have for lunch?"

The students were thrilled that Andrea asked that question. They knew Ms. Gray is a health food fan and that she runs marathons. Ms. Gray used this question as an opportunity to remind students to be healthy. "Well, I had yogurt, whole wheat bread, some blueberries, some almonds and some carrots, plus water. The absolutely perfect lunch!" Her smile was greeted with friendly groans and cordial laughter.

Ms. Gray continued the discussion about the survey before returning to what students had written as their description of lunch. "If you could advise our school's cafeteria manager, what ideas could come from the one quick survey we just took? Of course, more surveys involving more students would be necessary. Plus, the cafeteria has to follow many, many laws, regulations, policies, and rules. Still, in terms of business advice, what ideas could you offer the cafeteria based on or inspired by our one quick survey? Let's hear from everyone on this, so let's have another lightning round, quickly going down each row to hear from each of the young scholars here today. Michele, begin for us, please, then Christie and just keep going."

"People really like pizza."

"Have more variety of pizza."

"Have more variety of sandwiches."

"Have pizza every day."

"People like chicken nuggets."

"Have different sizes of salads."

"Have a super-size salad."

"Get fast-food pizza, not school pizza."

"Have more sauces for the chicken nuggets."

"Try some different sandwiches."

"Let us make our own sandwiches."

"Give a discount on two or three slices of pizza."

"Get some sauces for pizza."

"Pizza is always the favorite food."

"Get different chicken nuggets so we know it is chicken and not soy or something."

"Get bread sticks to go with pizza."

"My idea was already said. Maybe, well, maybe try toasting bread for the sandwiches. We do that at home."

"Get the super-thick pizza."

"Get the super-thin pizza."

"Get the vegetarian pizza so we can be healthy like Ms. Gray."

"Sell us the leftover pizza after school for snacks."

"Tell us a day before you have pizza so we can bring money for an extra slice."

"Get fast-food places to give you free samples of their new items for us to try."

"Don't just have cheese pizza."

"Have a way so people who bring their lunch to school don't have to wait in line just to buy milk."

After listening to all of the answers, Ms. Gray replied, "Great ideas. Wonderful thinking. Your suggestions could be very helpful to a school cafeteria or to other restaurants. Sally was typing your ideas. Of course, she was on the computer using word processing, but the old word typing still gets used. Sally you type faster than ever. Thanks for doing that word processing for us. When the cafeteria manger meets with our class tomorrow, she will be very impressed to get that printed list of outstanding ideas. Now, back to the original brain warm-up question. How was lunch? David, tell us."

"You know, it was just lunch, school lunch. I don't expect anything great. I do like pizza day. I bring an extra dollar on pizza day so I can get an extra slice. I have to pay for the extra slice myself, so I save a dollar from my allowance."

Six students had their hands up letting Ms. Gray know that they had ideas to share. Ms. Gray listed their names on the marker board in the order they would speak: Christie, William, Katie, Taylor, Anthony, and Matthew.

Christie's turn brought these thoughts: "You know, we have that infomercial project to do for this class. Well, I was thinking that the cafeteria needs an infomercial. It's probably a harder job than it looks to feed all of us. They have all of that food to buy. They cook for 600 or so people every day. They probably have a budget and have to save money to stay in their budget limits. So, you know, if the cafeteria made an infomercial and it was on school TV, maybe everyone would realize how tough the cafeteria job is."

William talked about lunch. "Lunch today was good actually. I like chicken nuggets. I tried that fruit salad and, well, I won't try that again. The chocolate pudding was good. The package it came in said low fat so I guess it is not too bad for us. I wanted an extra serving of chicken nuggets, but the cafeteria won't let you charge anything and I just had enough money for the price of lunch. I think they should let people charge, but I guess some people would never pay it back."

Katie was next. "Whenever they have a big salad, I get that. It's a full meal. I think it is, you know, pretty healthy and our health teacher gives us extra credit if we bring her one of those cafeteria stickers that say 'I was super healthy' today. You get one of those stickers when you get the big salad. The best part about that salad is you get a 50-cent discount. The regular lunch costs 50 cents more than the big salad, but the big salad is more food. I like saving the 50 cents."

Taylor had a different idea. "How was lunch? It was really bad. School pizza is nothing like real pizza. The chicken nuggets are not like real chicken. I just get peanut butter and jelly. At least it tastes like it is supposed to. I would suggest more sandwiches. Everyone likes sandwiches and there is nothing to cook."

Anthony had a creative idea. "I wonder if some of us could work in the cafeteria one day. We could see how their budget works. We could help unload a big shipment of food. We could help the cafeteria people. They really do have tough jobs and people never say 'thank you.' I liked lunch today. I think more people would appreciate lunch if they worked in the cafeteria one day."

Matthew completed the student input on the How was lunch? question. "I brought my lunch. I always do. My mom says it saves a little money, but the best part is I always like what I have for lunch. Plus, I don't have to wait in the lunch line. For people who don't like school lunch, just bring your own lunch."

Students are experts in lunch. By the time students are in middle school, they have gone to a school cafeteria over 1,000 times. This life experience provides many academic resources for an extreme economics teacher. Ms. Gray is not relying on an economics textbook or on worksheets that come with the textbook. Ms. Gray knows, just as Socrates did, that effective teaching and learning can come from a creative, logical, guided sequential process beginning with what a student knows and applying that as the initial step of a learning sequence that takes the student to mastery of new knowledge.

As a reality check, please think of the discussion Ms. Gray has had with her students in terms of the survey research results for this book and the list of basic economics vocabulary. How can the discussion of school lunch and additional applications of the school lunch topic connect with the survey results and the economics vocabulary?

The entire list of the economics vocabulary connects with lunch at school, but imagine that students were having trouble understanding the difference between two of those terms: *production* and *productivity*. How could the life experiences of students through years of eating lunch at school help those students understand the meaning of production, the meaning of productivity, and the differences between the two? Ms. Gray has an idea.

"The people who work in our school's cafeteria are involved each day in making lunch for over 600 students and teachers. The fancy word in economics for 'make' is *production*. Now, let's list everything we can think of that gets produced for lunch. The cafeteria workers do not grow the lettuce for a salad, but they do make the salad. Production of salads is part of getting lunch ready for everyone. Chopping up lettuce, slicing carrots, putting the salad in the plastic serving container are parts of the production of salads. Let's think of everything that is an example of production in the school cafeteria. Good, Fran, you start for

Table 9.1. Survey Results and Connections With School Lunch

Survey Results	*Connections With School Lunch*
1. Save, save more, keep saving	Save a dollar from allowance to buy extra slice of pizza.
2. Start saving now	Calculate the cost of a person bringing lunch to school versus buying lunch; expand those to a person bringing lunch to work throughout a career versus buying lunch each day.
3. Have a money plan	Calculate the cafeteria budget for (a) food costs and (b) revenue from customers.
4. Credit is deceptive	The cafeteria does not allow students to charge, that is, to eat now and pay later.
5. Live within your means	The extra slice of pizza costs a $1, which you either have saved and budgeted for or not.
6. Life is not about money	The economics class writing and discussion is about lunch, which captures the attention of all students. Ms. Gray will make the connections with money and with the overall economics curriculum.
7. Economics is measured by math	How much food needs to be ordered? What does the food in a lunch brought from home cost?
8. Get the best and the most education	Doing a day of job shadowing in the school cafeteria could be educational for students.
9. Develop a strong work ethic	Do the work to earn the money to be able to buy the extra slice of pizza.
10. People are more important than money	If you are not going to eat something you have on your tray at lunch, offer it to someone else.

us and then will just go down your row until we hear from everyone in the row."

"They make the menu each day."

"They make cookies."

"They have to increase production of pizza when the eighth graders get there. Eighth graders eat the most."

"They start production of lunch right after students finish breakfast."

"The cafeteria people are food production experts, and students are food consumption experts."

Ms. Gray was pleased. "Very good answers. *Production* means 'to make.' Now, let's imagine that one of the cafeteria workers is absent tomorrow due to illness. Six hundred students plus about 40 teachers and staff members will still go to lunch. There will be 7 cafeteria workers instead of 8, but the 7 people have to do all of the work that 8 people usually do. Productivity is about getting more work done in the same time as usual or in less time. What could the 7 cafeteria workers do tomorrow to increase their productivity, meaning to get more done with fewer workers but still feed everyone on time? Ernesto, you tell us, please, and then Angela, Christina, Jared, Sally, and Samantha."

"Make sure that each person does the job they do best."

"Check the menu and maybe serve something that is really easy to cook and put on trays."

"Don't cook anything for breakfast. Just have cereal and milk and bananas. That way, you know, there is nothing to clean up."

"Keep moving. Make sure that you are always getting something done."

"Help each other more. See who has the hardest job and who has the easiest job and help the person with the really hard job."

"Make sure that everyone knows exactly what to do. Tell people who is doing what part of the absent person's job. That way the stuff that has to get done will get done."

Ms. Gray was impressed. Now she hopes that a student could point out the difference between production and productivity. Shelby had a wonderful answer. "I know. Production of lunch happens every day. They make lunch every day. When someone is absent from cafeteria work, everyone else had to do more, produce more, I guess, than usual. Each worker's productivity has to go up when someone is absent."

Cara's hand was up and Ms. Gray smiled at her. "It's like my soccer team. We had two people absent from our last game. Our best goalie and our leading scorer were both absent, but we still won the game. Everyone who was at our game had to work harder and do more. It's like in the cafeteria if someone is absent."

Ms. Gray knew that the lunch discussions and applications were helping the students master the fundamentals of economics. The students' life experiences include years of lunch at school. The students' wholesome knowledge of, interest in, and talent with food is definite. Ms. Gray takes those responses and makes connections with economics, and by doing that, she causes learning.

How does an extreme economics teacher measure learning? The day-to-day discussions in class are part of the overall learning measurement system. Writing assignments in class such as the How was lunch? question can be collected and graded. Homework projects such as the infomercial can help measure learning. Tests are also important, so let's look at some test formats that an extreme economics teacher could use.

Economics First Test

Section 1:

__________ Rule 1 of economics

__________ Rule 2 of economics

__________ Rule 3 of economics

__________ A wonderful result for you if you follow Rules 1, 2, and 3 of economics

__________ What economics is all about—remember that life is about much more, but get the economics part of life right and the rest of life can be much better.

Section 2:

You make the smart decision to begin an IRA at age 22. You invest money so it earns 8% each year. That means your money will double every 9 years. Remember the rule of 72: The growth rate divided into 72 shows the number of years it takes for money to double. Now, complete the following calculations:

Age 22	$3,000 Money you deposit into your IRA
Age 31	______ How much that money has grown to
Age 40	______ How much that money has grown to
Age 49	______ How much that money has grown to
Age 58	______ How much that money has grown to
Age 67	______ How much that money has grown to

Section 3:

Draw your new design for the front side and the back of a new $1 coin.

Keep in mind, our government has tried in recent years to introduce $1 coins, but it has not worked. They looked too much like quarters. They did not vend in machines well. They did not seem "like a real dollar." In your design, prevent those problems.

Front of new $1 coin:

Back of new $1 coin:

What is the most important improvement you made that will cause your design to be accepted, used, and successful?

Economics core content vocabulary test

________	Interdependent	a. Nations together
________	Land, labor, capital	b. New, newer, newest
________	Scarcity	c. Maybe??
________	Advertisements	d. Do more with less
________	Finances	e. Better
________	Opportunity cost	f. Earth, work, money
________	Profit	g. Not enough
________	Risk	h. Amount: up, down, =
________	Supply and demand	i. Make money
________	Money	j. One
________	Competition	k. Commercials
________	Production	l. Money + price
________	Distribution	m. A or b, not both
________	Consumption	n. Use (consume)
________	Productivity	o. Deliver (distribute)
________	Specialize	p. Make (produce)
________	Technology	q. What economics is all about
Bonus: The three rules of economics:		r. $1,000,000

1. ____________ 2. ____________ 3. ____________

On the back of this test page write two paragraphs:

- One tells the good results that happen if you follow those three rules
- One tells the problems that would happen if you disobey those three rules

Economics Core Content and Three-Rules Test

____________	Produce more in less time, less work, and/or less energy
____________	What economics is all about
____________	One
____________	Earth, work, money
____________	Make money
____________	Make, produce
____________	Distribute, deliver

____________	Use, consume
____________	A or B, not both
____________	Up, down, balance; determines price; always true
____________	Commercials
____________	Not enough
____________	New, newer, newest
____________	People and nations working together
____________	Better
____________	= money + price
____________	Maybe?
____________	Three rules of economics

Part 1:
Think, think more, keep thinking
A restaurant decides to use a promotional offer in increase business and profit on Monday and Tuesday. The restaurant employees are encouraged to offer ideas. The best ideas will earn a $20 bonus for each of the employees who created the ideas. Five employees created five ideas, listed as follows:

1. For everyone who comes to the restaurant on Monday and buys a meal, you get a coupon for a free equal- or lesser-value meal on Tuesday.
2. When one adult pays for an adult meal, one child under 12 gets an equal- or lesser-value meal free.
3. A $100 drawing on Monday night and on Tuesday night. Everyone who eats at the restaurant on Monday may enter the drawing on Monday. Everyone who eats at the restaurant on Tuesday may enter the drawing on Tuesday.
4. You get to spin the wheel. The number the wheel lands on when you spin the wheel tells you the percentage price reduction to get on your total bill for Monday and Tuesday. The range is 10% to 50%.
5. Free dessert: You buy a meal, you select your free dessert.

Which of these five ideas do you think would do the most to reach the goals of increasing business at the restaurant on Monday and on Tuesday?

List two reasons why do you think that idea would work best.
1.
2.
Which of the five ideas do you think would do the least to reach the goals of increasing business and profit at the restaurant on Monday and Tuesday?
List two reasons why you think that idea would not work:
1.
2.

Economics core content vocabulary and doughnuts

1. _______ Making doughnuts
2. _______ Delivering doughnuts to grocery stores
3. _______ Eat doughnuts, eat more doughnuts, keep eating doughnuts
4. _______ Baking 100 doughnuts in 10 minutes; then baking 120 in 9 minutes with a new, improved recipe
5. _______ A new oven
6. _______ Grand opening today. Buy one dozen doughnuts, get one dozen free. Just bring the coupon from the newspaper. Limit one per customer. Now, back to our broadcast of the championship game.
7. _______ Chocolate or glazed doughnuts: the wheat/grain is from Kansas, the chocolate is from Switzerland, and the sugar is from South America.
8. _______ I have enough money to buy one chocolate doughnut or one glazed doughnut, but I don't have enough money for both.
9. _______ I got to the bakery at 9:45 on Saturday morning. They had only one dozen chocolate doughnuts left from the 50 they had at 6:00. There just are not enough. I need two dozen.
10. _______ With the money I have and the price of doughnuts, I have a problem with my _______.
11. _______ Here's a better offer. Buy one dozen doughnuts, get one doughnuts free, plus get today's newspaper free.
12. _______ Doughnuts, doughnuts, and doughnuts. Everything at this store is some type of doughnuts. They make one product—doughnuts.

13. ______ I was thinking of opening a new bakery, but maybe I would be successful and maybe not.
14. If I do open a new bakery, I will need a place for my business (a. ____________), I will need to work and hire other workers (b. ____________), and I will need a lot of money to invest to open the business (c. ____________).
15. ______ Okay, I can do this. I found a great location, I have hired the best doughnut cook in town, I have asked 1,000 people what they would like in a doughnut shop, and I am ready to give consumers what they have asked for. I can make money!
16. ______ The prices I can charge for my products will be determined by many factors, but nothing will be more important than this law.
17. ______ Even though this is what economics is all about, this is not what my new doughnut business is all about.

Bonus: If the doughnut shop is not all about money, what is it all about?

Circle each correct answer, one correct answer per question.

1. The word economics comes from an ancient Greek word that meant
   a. robot.
   b. computer.
   c. household management.
   d. Internet.
2. No matter what economics deals with—buying a car, getting a job, saving for college, paying bills—it always, always, always is concerned with
   a. learning how to speak different languages.
   b. money.
   c. the Super Bowl, the World Series, and popular movies.
   d. what food is served in middle school cafeterias.
3. In economics, there are many laws. One of the most important laws in economics is the law of
   a. obeying the speed limit on streets and highways.
   b. supply and demand.
   c. do not steal.
   d. attend school.

4. One job pays $8.00 an hour and another job pays $8.50 per hour. A person might decide to take the $8.00 job instead of the $8.50 job because
   a. the $8.00 job has many more benefits, such as 20% discounts for the employees who shop at the store.
   b. the $8.00 job is at a store that is one block from where you live so you never have to spend money to drive there.
   c. the $8.50 job is at a company that may go out of business in a few months.
   d. the $8.00 job guarantees an increase to $9.00 in 6 months.
5. True or false: It is smart, smart, and smart to save money whenever possible.
   a. True
   b. False

For the following multiple-choice questions, clearly circle the correct answer.

1. Rule 1 of economics is
   a. save.
   b. law of supply and demand.
   c. a = 3.14 times the radius squared.
   d. legislative, judicial, and executive.
2. Rule 2 of economics is
   a. beware of credit cards and the illusion of money they create.
   b. save more.
   c. individual retirement accounts can be started only when you are 35 years old or older.
   d. somebody is going to win the lottery, but almost everyone loses.
3. Rule 3 of economics is
   a. in every circle, the diameter times 3.14 equals the circumference.
   b. matter can exist as a liquid, solid or gas.
   c. keep saving.
   d. the latest blue jean design is an example of impressionistic art.
4. Economics is all about
   a. poetry, literature, and short stories.
   b. how to take a computer apart and put it back together again.

c. the stock market and nothing else.
d. money.

5. Now do the math for an individual retirement account investment of $3,000 made in the year 2015 that earns an average of 8%, which means that it will double every 9 years. Remember the rule of 72: the interest rate divided into 72 equals the number of years it takes for money to double—double, as in 2 becomes 4, then 4 becomes 8, then 8 becomes 16.

2015	$3,000	age 22
2024	$_____	age 31
2033	$_____	age 40
2042	$_____	age 49
2051	$_____	age 58
2060	$_____	age 67

Bonus: What would happen if that person could begin his or her IRA in 2006 at age 13?

We recently celebrated Presidents' Day. As you know, many coins and printed money are designed to have presidents of the United States pictured on them.

Design a new coin. Show the front and the back. Is a person on it? Who? What words are on it? What motto, phrase, or quote from U.S. history could be on it? What shape is it—there are reasons why coins are round, but you may have a better idea.

Front of the coin:

Back of the coin:

Economics core content

1. New, newer, newest
   a. black-and-white television sets
   b. radio or cassette tape players
   c. technology
   d. landing on the moon in July 1969
2. Not enough
   a. scarcity
   b. scare city

c. supply is greater than demand
d. prices going down to get rid of unsold 2006 model cars

3. Specialize
   a. "we sell everything for everyone"
   b. "no matter what you are looking for, we have it"
   c. a bakery
   d. Jeremy's Bar-B-Q and Quick Oil Change—eat while you wait to have your car serviced
4. Competition
   a. a charity
   b. one soft drink company versus another soft drink company
   c. members of the same soccer team
   d. employees of the same company
5. Productivity
   a. doing less in more time
   b. doing a little bit more in much more time
   c. doing more in less time
   d. doing nothing
6. Risk
   a. chances of winning the lottery
   b. money that you deposit in a bank savings account up to $100,000
   c. a bank certificate of deposit worth $10,000
   d. save, save more, keep saving
7. Production, distribution, consumption
   a. the three rules of economics
   b. make, deliver, use
   c. the three laws of supply and demand
   d. also known as the trio of capitalism, free market, and free enterprise
8. Advertise
   a. can be done only on television
   b. can be done only on radio
   c. can be done only in newspapers
   d. commercials
9. Opportunity cost
   a. A or B, not both
   b. A and a part of B, but not much

c. A and one-half of B now, one-half of B later
d. the price of a soft drink minus the calories

10. Law of supply and demand
    a. when the president of the United States changes prices
    b. up, down, balance; determines price; always true
    c. when the Congress of the United States changes prices
    d. when the Supreme Court of the United States changes prices
11. Money
    a. cannot be used to buy stocks
    b. cannot be used to rent a car
    c. what economics is all about
    d. can be used, but most people prefer to barter
12. Finances
    a. She did not buy the car, because the finances, the price of the car, and the money she had did not work out.
    b. He was able to get in shape for football by working out with finances.
    c. The only question on the college application from was about finances.
    d. The circumference divided by the diameter equals the finances of a circle.
13. Land, labor, capital
    a. the three rules of economics
    b. earth, homework, money
    c. nicknames of the three branches of the U.S. government
    d. earth, work, money
14. Profit
    a. to speak with much wisdom
    b. to get clothing made to perfectly fit you and only you
    c. to make money
    d. the cost of doing business is more than the income for the business
15. Interdependence
    a. This was written by Thomas Jefferson in 1776.
    b. This is what we celebrate on July 4.
    c. This describes people and nations working together.
    d. This is when the price is more than your budget can afford.

ECONOMICS: SILENT INDOOR-THINKING TEST

You decide to do with doughnuts what Starbucks has done with coffee. You will sell the most wonderful flavors of doughnuts, the most wonderful shapes and sizes for doughnuts, the most amazing variety of doughnuts, and you will sell these to customers in the most comfortable, attractive, and unique doughnut shop ever created.

1. What will you name your new store?
2. What are three reasons why that name is perfect for your new store?
   a.
   b.
   c.
3. List everything a customer will see when he or she walks into your store:
   a.
   b.
   c.
   d.
   e.
   f.
   g.
   h.
4. Write a 30-second radio commercial for your new store. Be sure to tell people what your store sells, where your store is located, the hours it is open, and what makes it worth the time and money for people to come here.
5. The local newspaper's critic (a person who evaluates or reviews a movie, a play, a book, or, in this case, a restaurant) visits your new doughnut store and brings two friends. The critic writes a summary of the new store and includes information about (a) the location, (b) the menu, (c) the appearance of the store, (d) the service provided by employees to customers, (e) the prices, and (f) the reasons that your store is better than or not better than your competition. In the space provided, write the restaurant critic's newspaper story about your new doughnut shop. Be sure to include all parts listed (a–f).

The variety of test formats serves many purposes, but two factors are consistent across the tests. One, I am measuring student achievement while I measure how well I have done my job. The tests help me confirm that all students have learned or reveal to me what still needs to be learned by which students. Two, the students can learn about economics as they read the questions and complete the tasks. Those tests are designed to continue the learning process. Students who ask me about when the next test will be often hear me reply, "We'll have a test when that is the best way for me to teach you."

In the past 4 years of extreme economics classes, students have never been told that a test would occur on a certain day. I am always confident that they will do well on tests. I have interacted with students during class to convince me that they have learned. Still, the written process is needed to accurately measure student achievement and teacher effectiveness.

The item listed as "first test" on pages 162 and 163 is usually given the second day of class. The students do well on that test and become aware of how capable they are.

Imagine that Ms. Gray and her students began class on a Monday with the How was lunch? activity. Please think of lessons that could be done each school day the rest of the week to extend the lunch case study or build on the lunch case study. For now, just an objective for the lesson and a few ideas for activities would be great. You can add the precise details later.

Tuesday

- Objective:
- Ideas for activities:
- Connections with students' life experience and wholesome knowledge, interests, and talents:

Wednesday

- Objective:
- Ideas for activities:
- Connections with students' life experience and wholesome knowledge, interests, and talents:

Thursday

- Objective:

- Ideas for activities:
- Connections with students' life experience and wholesome knowledge, interests, and talents:

Friday

- Objective:
- Ideas for activities:
- Connections with students' life experience and wholesome knowledge, interests, and talents:

Whether in elementary school, middle school, or high school, students have encountered economics in their life experiences. Students also have wholesome knowledge, interests, and talents that relate to, are affected by, and connect with economics. The extreme economics teacher uses these real-life resources to fascinate students, to apply existing motivations of students, and to cause learning. The extreme economics teacher gets to learn about students, about how current students learn, and about how to most effectively teach current students. The students get to learn economics, they get to learn that learning can be fascinating and real, and they get to team up with the teacher to create a classroom learning community. Everyone wins as everyone learns, learns more, and keeps learning.

The concluding chapter emphasizes what the research survey for this book confirmed that students need to know about economics.

10

SAVE. SAVE MORE. KEEP SAVING

Credit can be deceptive. Debt can be destructive. To prevent, avoid, and correct problems associated with credit or debt, there are three solutions: Save. Save more. Keep saving. No doubt, credit and debt have their defenders and their advocates. There are many more commercials encouraging people to spend money than there are any messages which encourage people to save money. This book willingly, eagerly, confidently communicates the less popular but more sensible option: Save. Save more. Keep saving.

The preface of this book deplores the debt disaster that the United States as a nation is imposing on itself and that Americans are imposing on themselves. Despite political rationalizations about debt as a percentage of anything and despite media reports of federal government officials justifying the national debt increasing from about $1 trillion in 1981 to $9 trillion in 2006, the reality is that credit can be deceptive and debt can be destructive.

Would the United States be in a stronger position internationally and domestically if the national government was debt free? Is a person in a stronger position if he or she is debt free? Yes and yes. How is the debt-free status reached? Save. Save more. Keep saving.

The purpose of this chapter is not to debate the political philosophies of fiscal or monetary policy, taxation, the money supply, deficit spending, or interest rate adjustments. Those issues are important, but they are the complex topics of other books.

The purpose of this chapter is to emphasize the fundamental concepts of economics that students need to master. The three most fundamental concepts are so essential about they are taught to my students during the initial minutes of the first class. These three essentials are repeated, discussed, explained, analyzed, ingrained, embedded, applied, learned, and mastered day after day, week after week, month after month. As stated earlier in this book, my students immediately memorize the words of these three short statements and permanently remember them: Save. Save more. Keep saving. Those are the three rules of economics.

The challenge is not to memorize those very few words. The challenge is to live up to those very big ideas. The research done for this book found that the most important financial advice that adults were eager to share with children and teenagers is, save money. Three years before the research for this book was done, I informally asked some successful adults to share with my students and me what they wish they had known about economics when they were in the eighth grade. Their top-ten list follows, with no surprise that the highest rated idea is to save money.

1. Develop the habit of saving—a certain amount on a certain schedule.
2. Use a budget.
3. Needs are top priority; wants are optional.
4. That item you just had to have and now never pay any attention to was not a good use of money.
5. Use the value and the power of compound interest.
6. Beware the trap of credit card debt.
7. Know and use the benefits of dollar cost averaging.
8. Save money early in life and enjoy big benefits later in life: The earlier money is saved, the more time it has to grow and grow and grow.
9. Save for and be responsible for your retirement income; do not expect to get anything from social security when you retire—if you do get something, it will be a bonus, but expect nothing.

10. A penny saved really is a penny earned because it is money you do not have to earn again to replace money spent.

There is no benefit to being obsessed with saving. Saving money is not presented as an obsession. People do consume products and services. Money does need to be spent on the necessities of life. Money should not be lost on wasteful, unnecessary expenditures. Students can develop wise judgment to understand the difference between needs and wants. The life experiences of students can apply to understanding this vital difference. "I wanted a new bicycle, but my father said the bike I have is all I need. Yeah, my bike works, but it's just not very cool. So if I save the money myself, I can get a new bicycle. I'm thinking of ways to make money. Maybe I'll save the money. My father would be so amazed."

Money is saved in many ways, including not spending, finding a better price, using what you have instead of buying something new, using coupons or other discounts, making an offer of a lower price, and eating meals and snacks at home instead of at restaurants or stores. "My mom said the ice cream place is too expensive. It would cost $8 if she and I went there for a snack. For just $3 or $4 she can buy a lot more ice cream at the grocery store. We get more ice cream for less money. That's the only way I'm going to get any ice cream, so that is fine with me."

Numbers can be convincing. Math is the measurement system and is part of the language for economics, so having students work with real numbers can be persuasive and enlightening. The chart that follows shows students the real numbers associated with money that is left alone to grow. The students calculate each cell/number in the chart and really feel the money totals grow, and they are amazed that 8% or 9% growth over 5 years surpasses the 3% of growth of 13 years; however, if the 9% rate of return has a larger risk, such as that of stocks, and the 9% is an overall average of good and bad years, some students then prefer the slow, steady 3% or 4% with a bank-guaranteed account. What other topics could you and your students discuss based on the calculations and numbers on Table 10.1?

Table 10.1. The Power of Compound Interest

	3%	4%	8%	9%
Begin	$3,000	$3,000	$3,000	$3,000
1 year later	3,090	3,120	3,240	3,270
2 years later	3,183	3,245	3,499	3,564
3 years later	3,278	3,375	3,779	3,885
4 years later	3,377	3,510	4,081	4,235
5 years later	3,478	3,650	4,408	4,616
6 years later	3,582	3,796		
7 years later	3,690	3,948		
8 years later	3,800	4,106		
9 years later	3,914	4,270		
10 years later	4,032	4,441		
11 years later	4,153			
12 years later	4,277			
13 years later	4,406			

Conclusions:
Interest = the price of ________________
Compound interest = ________________
Rate of return = growth on an investment

The students and I often revisit the three rules of economics: Save. Save more. Keep saving. We chant these rules, but we explore, analyze, explain, implement, learn, and master these rules. Some students ask about get-rich schemes they have heard about, such as "work at home and make $6,000 per month"; "win the lottery and you are an instant millionaire"; "just buy our tapes and instruction system, plus a 3-month supply of our nutritional supplements and you're in business with the potential for tens of thousands of dollars of easy profit." We analyze the facts about those schemes and identify the flaws in each scheme. The following list is one part of the analysis we do.

1. Save. Save more. Keep saving:
   Chances of you earning money:
   Chances of you losing money:
2. Lottery:
   Chances of winning money:
   Chances of losing money:
   Chances of the lottery organization making money:

3. Bank:
   Chances of you earning money:
   Chances of you losing money:
   Chances of the bank making money:
4. Stock market:
   Chances of you earning money:
   Chances of you losing money:
   Chances of the company/companies making money:

Students are well aware of commercials, but few commercials encourage people to actually save money. The television advertisement that says, "0% interest for one year. No payment for 6 months. Shop today. Buy today. Pay later," is not about saving money. The tiny print on the TV screen at the end of that commercial explains enough conditions and disclaimers to make any wise consumer flee. The following activity applies the life experience of students as viewers of commercials in a creative way to help them master the reasons and ways to save, save more, keep saving.

ECONOMICS HOMEWORK PROJECT

Part 1: Save. Save more. Keep saving. You will create a 60-second TV or radio commercial about the idea of Save. Save more. Keep saving. The commercials will be broadcast at our school on the TV news or the public address system. The goals of the commercial are to convince middle school students and high school students to save, save more, keep saving and to tell middle school students and high school students many ways to save, save more, keep saving. Write the script here or on notebook paper very, very neatly. If it is a TV script, describe the video. If it is a radio script, describe the setting and any sound effects you use.
TV or radio (circle one)
* the words that are heard * the video or the setting *
Scene 1:
Scene 2:
Scene 3:
Scene 4:

Part 2: Design the logo of the Save. Save more. Keep saving. communication campaign. The logo can be all picture/drawing graphic or a combination of picture and words.

Sometimes, when the students continue working on the three rules, our work is rudimentary. Sports teams practice the same drills and plays until the repetition brings perfection. Economics students can also benefit from drill and repetition as part of the overall learning process. The following activity as a class warm-up to begin the day's work, as a quiz, as part of a test, or as a frequent chant/repletion can serve such purposes.

Rule 1 of economics:
Rule 2 of economics:
Rule 3 of economics:
Two good results if you follow Rules 1, 2 and 3 of economics:
1.
2.
What economics is all about:

Note: Life is about much more than money—family, friends, commitments, achievements, helping people, and more—but if you get the money part of life managed well, it helps the other parts of life go much better.

The rule of 72: Divide the rate of return, such as an interest rate or the rate at which an investment is gowning, into 72 to calculate how many years are needed for money to double.

Use a rate of return of 8% in this IRA calculation:

2005	$3,000	your age now:
2014		your age then:
2023		your age then:
2032		your age then:
2041		your age then:
2050		your age then:
2059		your age then:
2068		your age then:

Question: So, if you keep doing this with $3,000 more in years 2006, 2007, and so on, what would the result be after several decades?

Actions get results. The extreme economics classroom is an active place where results are plentiful, continual, and required. The capitalist economic system thrives on designed, intentional, purposeful, ethical, legal actions. My students are taught that a proper work ethic is expected and will be demonstrated in daily class work, in class discussions, in homework projects, in high levels of participation and attention.

Students sometimes respond well to stories. The following story was written for my eighth graders to help convince them of the importance of establishing the habit of eagerly working hard now. "Work, work more, keep working" is how the standard is sometimes communicated.

"I'LL SHOW YOU"

"I know, I know. I could make better grades. It's just no big deal. I could probably make all As and Bs. Honor roll would be easy. It always was, but what's the point? I'll still get into college and I'll do better then. There are other things to do now." Shawn sounded comfortable with his C grades and his C attitude. His twin sister, Tasha, was not convinced.

"Come on, Shawn. Get real. You always made the honor roll in middle school. I did my best then to keep up with you. Now, I make straight As or maybe a B now and then. You just get by. You do enough to stay out of serious trouble. Cs, come on Shawn, you can do better than that. It's that group you hang out with. The 'we hate school' group or the 'school is stupid' group or whatever you call yourselves." Tasha's frustration and disappointment were genuine.

"Back off, Tasha. I do okay. Who asked you for a sermon? I'll get into just as many colleges as you do. Why should I work so hard in high school? My friends and I have lots of fun. I never make a D grade. I've become the expert in making easy Cs. Ninth grade was great—people to meet and things to do. I'm not going to study all the time like some people do. Tenth grade is the same. Next year I'll get a part-time job and buy a car. Then I'll do really well on the SAT. Colleges will love me. And those friends of mine who agree with me about school, we'll get together and design websites. We've made money doing that and it is so easy to do. Why study when I can make money?"

Tasha did not know about the money. "No way," she replied with a slight hint of jealousy.

"Yeah, Jason's father pays us to update his company's website each day. Thirty minutes of work and we each get $50 a week. How's that for success? While you study and make As we work, get paid, and make Cs.

Who needs grades when you have a job?" Shawn seemed quite pleased with himself.

Sometimes Tasha wondered about that question—who needs grades when you have a job?—when she spent extra time studying.

About a year later, in June of the summer after their junior year of high school, Tasha and Shawn got their SAT scores. Tasha's score put her in the top 10% of the country. Shawn's score was, well, it was right in the middle. He made C grades and he scored in the middle on the SAT.

"Dumb test. Who cares about the scores? Maybe I don't need college after all. Who cares?" Shawn was not very convincing.

Tasha had heard enough from her brother. "You care. You've wasted 3 years of high school. You and Jason thought you'd get rich working on websites. Then Jason's father fired both of you for that silly stuff you put on the website one time. Then you quit your fast-food job because you said the work was too hard. Now what are you going to do?"

Shawn began to argue. "Who put you in charge of me? I know what . . ."

Tasha stopped him. "I put me in charge of you. I'm tired of people at school asking me what happened to Shawn. It's embarrassing to hear people ask why you goof off so much. Your loser friends keep coming over to the house or calling. I don't want to be seen with them. You let that group bring you down. Your grades. The SAT. Your jobs. Don't you get it, Shawn? You are better than that. Make something out of your senior year."

Shawn was thinking. "Like what? What can I do?"

"You used to run track in middle school. You worked on the yearbook and you did morning TV announcements at school then. Mom and Dad have taken your cell phone, your car they got for you, and your computer. They hired tutors for you. They gave you freedom and you blew that."

After a long moment of silence, Shawn asked, "Well, what can I do now? It's June. We'll be seniors in August. What can I do now?"

Tasha's answer was not what Shawn expected to hear. "Run. Start running today. I have to run on my own for soccer training. Some girls from the team and I run every night about 8. Start running with us and then get on the cross-country team. Go to school tomorrow and get your schedule changed. Take some real classes, not all of those play classes you signed up for. Check the websites to see what summer reading serious seniors will be doing and read—you know, open a book and read it."

Shawn was taking his sister's advice seriously. "How'd you learn all about this?" Shawn asked.

"I pay attention, Shawn. I listen to teachers just like you used to. I listen to Mom and Dad. They are smarter than you think. I study. How long has it been since you did that?"

"Yeah, it's been a long time, I guess. You and I really did well in elementary shool and middle school. We won all kinds of awards. I guess I've been pretty dumb, huh?"

Tasha replied loudly. "Pretty dumb! You've been super dumb. To be as smart as you are, you've been crazy dumb. You wasted 3 years of high school, so our senior year is your last chance. Go to school right now and change your schedule. Be ready to run tonight with three soccer superstars who you can't keep up with."

Shawn jumped up at that comment. "Sounds like a challenge to me. You're on. Think you and your soccer friends can keep up with me? I'll show you."

Tasha smiled and left Shawn's room. She turned around and made one final encouraging comment as only a confident, conscientious teenager could. "I'll outrun you tonight, but I'll be just as happy when you outrun me, if you ever do."

"If . . . if I ever do?" Shawn spoke with feelings this time. I'll outrun you and I'll make better grades than you. I'll show you, Tasha." That was Tasha's hope.

One month later Shawn and Tasha ran in the local 10,000-meter race. Her time was 46:17 and his time was 47:23. One month later they ran in a 5,000-meter race. His time was 22:27 and her time was 22:37. One year later Tasha and Shawn both had senior-year grade point averages over 3.8, with hers of 3.86 and his of 3.82. Shawn's SAT and ACT scores were now much better. Tasha had decided on a nearby university, where she would study biology and after that go to medical school. Shawn had decided to attend a college about 25 miles away and become a high school teacher so he could help high school students avoid the mistakes he had made. Shawn had shown Tasha a lot, but he had shown himself a lot more.

Economics is all about money. Life is about much more than money. If you manage the money part of life well, the other parts of life can be greatly enhanced.

Our nation is setting a bad financial example for children and teenagers. National debt and personal debt are excessive. The nation is not saving money. Many individuals save little or no money. If these bad habits continue, financial difficulties or disasters will occur throughout our society, throughout our communities, in our families. Such financial failure is not necessary, but to prevent it, serious disciplined actions are needed.

Can education help? Yes, but education alone is insufficient. People have been educated about the health problems associated with tobacco for decades, but tobacco products are still consumed. People have been educated about the importance of physical exercise and eating healthy foods, but the percentage of seriously overweight Americans is alarming.

Yes, education can help. Effective education about economics can help. When that education is provided by and experienced through the extreme economics approach, the impact can increase because what is learned is real, is personal; it connects right here and right now to the life the person being educated is living.

Overall, the adults in the United States are setting a counterproductive example about money management, saving, and economics. The adults in the country are responsible for a national debt of $9 trillion. The adults in this country are responsible for a Social Security system that overpromises and cannot be sustained. Far too many of the adults in this country are not saving money for retirement, for emergencies, or for the type of items that earlier generations saved for but recent generations borrow for.

Some adults set a superior example about saving, about money management, about economics. Some families use a budget and teach their children to use a budget. Those children experience the reality that no money in the entertainment fund means not going to the movies, so create a game, read a book, earn some money. Given the realities of our nation's financial irresponsibility and our national savings rate being low, the adults who are setting a good example must not be in the majority.

Education can play a vital role in solving economic problems. Schools are already asked to resolve many issues, educational and other, that children and teenagers face. Adding the task of teaching extreme economics to the already crowded curriculum at schools may be difficult, but there are possibilities. In schools, school districts, and states that already have economics in the curriculum, make sure that what is taught and how it is taught results in students having the knowledge and the skills to manage money. Extreme economics is one way to get that result.

In all schools, existing subjects other than economics could connect with learning about money. Rather than enduring page after page and worksheet after worksheet of ordinary math problems, students could do money math. When learning about percentages, the math problems could include calculations about money saved when a product is discounted 20%, 40%, or 50%. Interest rates could be the topic of math percentages. If students saw more practical application of math to their lives now, such as money math, they could make a stronger commitment to math, they could learn more math, and they could simultaneously learn economics.

History classes also provide many opportunities for connections with economics. American history includes debates about the banking system, purchase of land from other countries, taxation, paper money, the gold and silver standard, how to pay for war expenses, and other topics that relate to economics vocabulary, to economics concepts, and to money.

The operation of a school itself presents an economics case study that a school's computer class could use. A public school's budget—textbooks and other instructional supplies, athletics, various departments, fund-raising projects, the cafeteria, vending machines, government funding for specific purposes, and other financial matters—is public information. These data could be organized by students in a computer class to master financial software, spreadsheets, and fundamentals of computer programs. Why use ordinary, generic data when real data from the students' school can make the learning experience much more meaningful and real?

We know what works. That statement of truth and confidence is a fundamental idea in each book I have written about teaching. We know what works in education, in teaching, in the classroom. We know what causes learning. We know what highly effective teachers do.

In personal economics, we know what works. We know what causes financial success. We know the benefits of Save. Save more. Keep saving. We know the wise insights of financial lessons learned by the people who provided input to the research done for this book.

We know what works in teaching. We know what works in economics. Combine those conclusions to realize that we know what works in teaching economics.

Extreme economics presents a method, an approach, a perspective on teaching economics. Extreme economics is based on 10 years of research and writing about highly effective teaching. Extreme economics is based on classroom experiences during 4 years in which each student made a grade of A or B in eighth-grade economics classes. Extreme economics is also based on research that indicates what children and teenagers need to know about money. Extreme economics explains and demonstrates how to teach children and teenagers about money so learning is caused.

About 40 years ago, my grandfather and I were taking a walk. We discussed several topics. During the discussion he said to me, "Keen, you need to save 10 cents every day so when you need new tires for a car you will have the money you need." My grandfather's wisdom is timeless. He grew up in a very thrifty household. His father was a circuit-riding Methodist minister in western Kentucky. The family income was quite limited, so the family faith had to be unlimited and the family frugality had to be continuous.

In 1939 my grandfather Keen Johnson became governor of Kentucky. He promised to be a "saving, thrifty, frugal" governor. The printed stationary of the previous governor was used by my grandfather, who simply drew a line through the name of this predecessor, "Happy" Chandler, and wrote in the name Keen Johnson.

During their terms in office—1930s depression years and World War II years—Governors Chandler and Johnson eliminated Kentucky's budget debt so effectively that when Governor Johnson left office in 1943, the state had a financial surplus.

How was that done? One dime at a time, just as he advised me to save money for new tires one dime at a time. The mentality that "each dime counts so count each dime" leads to the action of saving every dime possible. My grandfather's first thought about money was to save. Unfortunately, saving money seems to be the last thought about money that our country has now and that many people in our country have now.

Debt can be destructive. Excessive debt can destroy an individual, a family, a business, an organization, a country.

The scope of this book has not included sophisticated stock market investment strategies or the intracies of international currency fluctuations. There are many other books that properly address in precise detail the many subtopics within economics.

The scope of this book is to identify what children and teenagers need to know about money and to present a teaching approach that, when used effectively by teachers or parents/guardians, will help cause children and teenagers to learn about money.

We conclude with the three rules of economics. Follow these rules and you win financially. Of course, life is about more than money, finances, or economics, but getting the money part of life managed wisely will enhance the other parts of life.

Let's all chant together. The three rules of economics are Save. Save more. Keep saving. Imagine the results that can be obtained by our country and by our citizens if as a society and as individuals we wisely save, save more, keep saving. My grandfather and his generation knew the necessity, the virtue, the wisdom, the benefits, the discipline of saving. The future of this country and the futures for our children and teenagers will be enhanced by applying wisdom from the past that was confirmed by the research for this book: Save. Save more. Keep saving.

That may sound like an extreme idea, which helps make it a perfect foundation for extreme economics.

ABOUT THE AUTHOR

Keen Babbage has taught social studies in grades 7–12 and education classes at the college and graduate levels. He has school administration experience with grades 6–12 and has executive experience with three large corporations. He is the author of *911: The School Administrator's Guide to Crisis Management* (1996), *Meetings for School-Based Decision Making* (1997), *High-Impact Teaching: Overcoming Student Apathy* (1998), *Extreme Teaching* (2002), *Extreme Learning* (2004), *Extreme Students: Challenging All Students and Energizing Learning* (2005), and *Results-Driven Teaching: Teach So Well That Every Student Learns* (2006), all from Rowman & Littlefield Education.

www.ingramcontent.com/pod-product-compliance
Ingram Content Group UK Ltd.
Pitfield, Milton Keynes, MK11 3LW, UK
UKHW041104150926
475561UK00001BA/28

9 781578 865642